SILVER·BURDETT

Making Music

Program Authors

Jane Beethoven
Susan Brumfield
Patricia Shehan Campbell
David N. Connors
Robert A. Duke
Judith A. Jellison

Rita Klinger
Rochelle Mann
Hunter C. March
Nan L. McDonald
Marvelene C. Moore
Mary Palmer
Konnie Saliba

Will Schmid
Carol Scott-Kassner
Mary E. Shamrock
Sandra L. Stauffer
Judith Thomas
Jill Trinka

PEARSON

Scott
Foresman

Editorial Offices: Glenview, Illinois • Parsippany, New Jersey • New York, New York
Sales Offices: Parsippany, New Jersey • Duluth, Georgia • Glenview, Illinois
Coppell, Texas • Ontario, California • Mesa, Arizona

ISBN: 0-382-36571-2

Contributing Authors

Audrey A. Berger
Roslyn Burrough
J. Bryan Burton
Jeffrey E. Bush
John M. Cooksey
Shelly C. Cooper
Alice-Ann Darrow
Scott Emmons
Debra Erck
Anne M. Fennell
Doug Fisher
Carroll Gonzo
Larry Harms
Martha F. Hilley
Debbie Burgoon Hines

Mary Ellen Junda
Donald Kalbach
Shirley Lacroix
Henry Leck
Sanna Longden
Glenn A. Richter
Carlos Xavier Rodriguez
Kathleen Donahue Sanz
Julie K. Scott
Gwen Spell
Barb Stevanson
Kimberly C. Walls
Jackie Wiggins
Maribeth Yoder-White

Listening Map Contributing Authors

Patricia Shehan Campbell
Jackie Chooi-Theng Lew
Ann Clements
Kay Edwards
Sheila Feay-Shaw
Kay Greenhaw

David Hebert
Hunter C. March
Carol Scott-Kassner
Mary E. Shamrock
Sandra L. Stauffer

Movement Contributing Authors

Judy Lasko
Marvelene C. Moore
Dixie Piver

Wendy Taucher
Susan Thomasson
Judith Thompson-Barthwell

Recording Producers

Buryl Red, Executive Producer

Rick Baitz
Rick Bassett
Bill and Charlene James
Joseph Joubert
Bryan Louiselle
Tom Moore

J. Douglas Pummill
Michael Rafter
Mick Rossi
Buddy Skipper
Robert Spivak
Jeanine Tesori
Linda Twine

Contents
Steps to Making Music

☆ = **Core Lesson**

👆 = **Reading Sequence**

Core Lesson =

Reading Sequence =

★ = **Core Lesson**

✊ = **Reading Sequence**

Unit 4 Building Our Musical Skills 120

Unit Introduction

Core Lesson =
Reading Sequence =

= **Core Lesson**

= **Reading Sequence**

Core Lesson =

Reading Sequence =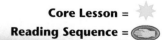

Paths to Making Music

Unit 11 Tuneful Tales · · · · · · · · · · · · · · · · · · 348
Unit Introduction

Unit 12 Holidays to Share · · · · · · · · · · · · · · 374
Unit Introduction

Music Resources and Indexes

STEPS TO
Making
Music

How to Say Hello

Did you feel shy on your first day of school? Did you meet old friends from last year? Sometimes it's hard to say hello to people you haven't met. Making music is a way to find new friends as you play together.

Read this poem and imagine how you can say hello to people who may become new friends.

Hello to the World
by Susan Katz

The sunshine sings HELLO
each morning as it greets the sky.
And wherever we happen to be
in the world, we smile
as each ray makes its way
in a golden HELLO
through our window.

Sing HELLO to the millions of children
who are dreaming of someone like you.
They hope to hear your HELLO in their ears
so their worlds can become united as one
with your world, and the loving embrace
of your friendly HELLO will be worn
by the world like a smile on a face.

Poetry in Motion

Create an eight-beat pattern by patting your legs and brushing your hands together. **Perform** your pattern between the stanzas of the poem.

2

Let the Music Begin!

How to Say Hello

Children all over the world have a lot in common. They play games and sing songs. **Listen** to this song to hear greetings in nine languages! Then you can **sing** along.

CD 1–1

Hello to All the Children of the World

Words by Nancy Klein

Music by Nancy Klein and Pam Beall

REFRAIN

Hel - lo, *Bon-jour, Bue-nos dí - as,* G' - day, *Gu-ten Tag, Kon-ni-chi wa.*

Ciao, Sha-lom, Do-brey dy - en, Hel - lo to all the child-ren of the world!

VERSE

1. We live in dif - f'rent plac - es from all a - round the world.
2. There's child - ren in the des - erts, and child - ren in the towns

We speak in man - y dif - f'rent ways. __
And child - ren who live by the sea. ____

Though some things might be dif - f'rent, we're child - ren just the same,
If we could meet each oth - er to run and sing and play,

D. C. al Fine

And we all like to sing and play.
Then what good friends we all and could be.

Dynamic

Move to show the **dynamics** in the song. Bounce your heels to the beat as you do each of these movements.

The louds and softs in music are called **dynamics**.

p

mp

mf

f

Moves

Watch the Signs

Look for the signs in the music that tell you when to sing loudly and when to sing softly. The signs are called dynamic marks. What do you think *mf* and *mp* mean?

p = *piano* = soft

f = *forte* = loud

CD 1–3
MIDI 1

Supercalifragilisticexpialidocious

(from *Mary Poppins*)

Words and Music by Richard M. Sherman and Robert B. Sherman

p
Sup - er - cal - i - frag - il - is - tic - ex - pi - al - i - do - cious!

mp
E - ven though the sound of it is some-thing quite a - tro - cious,

mf
If you say it loud e - nough, you'll al - ways sound pre - co - cious.

Fine

f
Sup - er - cal - i - frag - il - is - tic - ex - pi - al - i - do - cious!

p
Um did - dle did - dle did - dle, um did - dle ay!

Um did - dle did - dle did - dle, um did - dle ay!

1. Be-cause I was a-fraid to speak when I was just a lad,

Me fa-ther gave me nose a tweak and told me I was bad.

But then one day I learned a word that saved me ach-in' nose,

The big-gest word you ev-er 'eard and this is 'ow it goes: Oh!

2. 'E traveled all around the world and ev'rywhere 'e went
'E'd use his word and all would say, "There goes a clever gent!"
When dukes and maharajas pass the time of day with me,
I say me special word and then they ask me out to tea. Oh! *Refrain*

3. So when the cat has got your tongue, there's no need for dismay.
Just summon up this word and then you've got a lot to say.
But better use it carefully or it can change your life.
One night I said it to me girl and now me girl's me wife. Oh! *Refrain*

Sing It Out!

What dynamics does Julie Andrews use to sing *In My Own Little Corner?*

CD 1–5

In My Own Little Corner

**From *Cinderella*
by Richard Rodgers and Oscar Hammerstein**

The musical *Cinderella* was written especially for television.

M·U·S·I·C M·A·K·E·R·S
Julie Andrews

Julie Andrews (born 1935) studied tap and ballet dancing as a young girl in England. It was soon discovered that she had a wonderful voice. She started singing lessons at the age of eight and had her first musical role when she was twelve. When she was thirteen years old, she performed for the King and Queen of England. Andrews has appeared in many musicals and movies. Among the most popular were *My Fair Lady, Mary Poppins,* and *The Sound of Music*.

What's in a Name? RHYTHM!

You've got rhythm. You've also got the beat. When you clap your hands or tap your foot to a song, are you clapping the **beat** or the **rhythm?**

Say the words of this speech piece while patting your knees to the steady beat.

The **beat** is the regular pulse felt in most music.

Rhythm is a pattern of long and short sounds and silences.

CD 1–6

Name, Name, What's Your Name?

Name, name, what's your name? Say it now, we'll play a game.

Say it high, say it low, an-y old way, but don't be slow.

Ellen

Carlos

Names to Play

Different names can have different rhythms.
Look at the examples below.

1. Pra – nav, Pra – nav

2. Joe, Joe

3. Mar – i – sol, Mar – i – sol

What rhythm do you hear in your name?

Rhythms to Play

Play these rhythm patterns with
"Name, Name, What's Your Name?"
Choose a rhythm instrument for each pattern.

William Shakespeare wrote, "What's in a name? That which we call a rose by any other name would smell as sweet." What do you think he meant?

Playing with Rhythms

This song from Trinidad has different rhythms.

One sound on a beat =

Two sounds on a beat =

No sounds on a beat =

Look for these rhythms as you **sing** "Gypsy in the Moonlight."

CD 1–8

Gypsy in the Moonlight

Folk Song from Trinidad

do

F   C₇

1. Gyp - sy   in   the   moon - light,   Gyp - sy   in   the   dew,
2. Walk   in,   gyp - sy,   walk   in,   Walk right   in   I   say,

C₇   F

Gyp - sy   ne - ver   come   back   un - til   the   clock strikes two.
Walk   in - to   my   par - lor   to   hear   the   ban - jo   play.

4. Tra-la-la . . .

3. I don't want nobody,
   Nobody wants me,
   All I want is Mary
   to come and dance with me.

Speaking Rhythm

Read and **perform** these rhythms. Then find them in "Gypsy in the Moonlight."

Now find both rhythm patterns in "Alligator Pie."

CD 1–10

Alligator Pie

Poem by Dennis Lee

Rhythmic Setting by Edith Bicknell

Al - li - ga - tor pie,   al - li - ga - tor pie,

If I don't get some I think I'm gon - na die.

Give a - way the green grass, give a - way the sky, But

don't give a - way my al - li - ga - tor pie.

Create your own four beat rhythm pattern using ♩ , ♫ , and 𝄾 .

Four Sounds on a Beat

Rhythms come in many combinations.
Here's a song with a new one!

CD 1–15

Ding, Dong, Diggidiggidong

English Version Adapted by Margaret Murray

From Orff-Keetman, Orff-Schulwerk, Vol. 1

Ding, dong, dig-gi-dig-gi-dong, Dig-gi-dig-gi-dong, the cat she's gone.

Ding, dong, dig-gi-dig-gi-dong, Dig-gi-dig-gi-ding dang dong.

Which four syllables have four sounds on a beat?

Ding,   **dong,**   **dig-gi-dig-gi-**   **dong,**

The rhythm that has four sounds on a beat looks like this: ♩♫♫

Sing the song and point to the notes as you sing. Find each ♩♫♫ in the song.

Sing the song again with rhythm syllables as you clap the rhythm.

Tune In

Folklore tells us cats have nine lives. Actually, their spines are very flexible, so they can twist to land on their feet and escape danger.

Cats
(excerpt)
by Eleanor Farjeon

Cats sleep
Anywhere,
Any table,
Any chair,
Top of piano,
Window-ledge,
In the middle,
On the edge.

Hear the Bells

Listen to another version of "Ding, Dong, Diggidiggidong." How is it different from the way you sang it?

CD 1–22

Ding, Dong, Diggidiggidong

from Orff-Keetman, *Orff-Schulwerk, Vol. 1*

This version is accompanied by xylophone, cello, and timpani.

Show What You Know!

Sing this pattern with rhythm syllables first. Then **sing** the pitch syllables. Now **sing** the words while you **play** the pattern on a xylophone.

mi   mi   mi   mi   re   mi   do
dig-gi-dig-gi-ding dang dong.

Ring Around the New Rhythm

Sing "Golden Ring Around Susan Girl."

Find the new rhythm with four sounds on a beat in this song. **Read** and **perform** the verse of the new song using rhythm syllables.

 CD 1–23

Golden Ring Around Susan Girl

Folk Song from the Appalachian Mountains
as sung by Jean Ritchie

Gold - en ring a - round the Su - san girl,

Gold - en ring a - round the Su - san girl,

Gold - en ring a - round the Su - san girl,

All the way a - round our Su - san girl.

Moving Rhythms

Read each of the rhythms using rhythm syllables.

1.

2.

3.

Create your own rhythm using [quarter note], [two eighth notes], [quarter rest], and [four sixteenth notes].

Play your rhythm pattern by snapping, patting, stamping, or clapping. How many ways can you play your rhythm?

Listening for Rhythms

Pat a steady beat as you **listen** to Jean Ritchie sing *Golden Ring Around the Susan Girl*.

Find the [four sixteenth notes] in the song.

CD 1–25

Golden Ring Around the Susan Girl

Folk Song from the Appalachian Mountains as performed by Jean Ritchie

This version is accompanied by banjo and dulcimer.

◀ banjo

▲ dulcimer

Same Same **Different** Same

This French song has four lines of music. Each line is a **phrase**. **Sing** to discover which of the phrases in *"Au clair de la lune"* sound alike. Do they look alike, too?

A **phrase** is a musical sentence.

CD1 1–26
MIDI 2

Au clair de la lune
(In the Moonlight)

English Version by D. Auberge

Traditional Song from France

Au   clair   de   la   lu - ne,   Mon   a - mi   Pier - rot,
Stand-ing   in   the   moon - light,   Mon   a - mi   Pier - rot,

Prê - te - moi   ta   plu - me,   Pour   é - crire   un   mot;
I   have   lost   my   can - dle,   How,   I   do   not   know!

Ma   chan - delle   est   mor - te   je   n'ai   plus   de   feu.
If   you   can - not   help   me,   I   will   have   to   stay

Ou - vre - moi   ta   por - te,   Pour   l'a - mour   de   Dieu.
Stand-ing   in   the   dark - ness,   'til   the   light   of   day.

Follow the Phrases

Listen for the phrases that are alike as you follow the listening map.

CD 1–30

Ah, vous dirai-je, Maman

**from *12 Variations in C, K. 265/300e*
by Wolfgang Amadeus Mozart**

Mozart [MOHT-zahrt] based this piano piece on a French folk song. You may know this song as "Twinkle, Twinkle, Little Star."

Element: FORM   **Skill: MOVING**   **Connection: CULTURE**

Unlock the Form

How many sections do you see in this song?
Listen to find the **form.**

Form is the overall plan of a piece of music.

CD 1–31
MIDI 3

Ambos a dos
(Go Two by Two)

English Words by Aura Kontra   *Folk Song from Latin America*

A

Am - bos   a   dos,   ma - ta - ri - le,   ri - le,   ri - le,
Go   two   by   two,   *ma - ta - ri - le,   ri - le,   ri - le,*

Am - bos   a   dos,   ma - ta - ri - le,   ri - le,   ron.
Go   two   by   two,   *ma - ta - ri - le,   ri - le,   ron.*

B

1.   Yo ten - go un   cas - ti - llo,   ma - ta - ri - le,   ri - le,   ri - le,
1.   Come in - to   my   cas - tle,   *ma - ta - ri - le,   ri - le,   ri - le,*

Yo ten - go un   cas - ti - llo,   ma - ta - ri - le,   ri - le,   ron,   pon,   pon.
Come in - to   my   cas - tle,   *ma - ta - ri - le,   ri - le,   ron,   pon,   pon.*

2. ¿Dónde están las llaves? . . .
    ¿Dónde están las llaves? . . .

2. Where's the key to the door? . . .
    Where's the key to the door? . . .

Play with Form

Play this part on your recorder when you hear the **A** section.

Move to the Form

The pictures show one way to play a game with this song. **Move** to show the two different sections in the song.

Did I hear a violin on that recording?

A ▼ March in place to the beat of the music.

B Twist from right to left to the beat of the music. ▶

Joyful Form

Find the words *verse* and *refrain* in this song. Most songs that have a verse and refrain are **A** **B** form. **Sing** "Joy to the World." The verse can be sung as a solo. Everyone can join in on the refrain.

CD 1–35

Joy to the World

Words and Music by Hoyt Axton

A **VERSE**

do

1. Jer-e-mi-ah was a bull _ frog, Was a good friend of mine. _

_____ Nev-er un-der-stood a sin-gle word he said, _

but we al-ways had a might-y fine time. _

Yes, we al-ways had a might-y fine time.

22

B REFRAIN

Sing-ing joy to the world. All ___ the boys and girls _ now.

Joy to the fish-es in the deep blue sea. _ Joy to you and me. __

2. If I were the king of the world,
   Tell you what I'd do,
   Throw away the fears and the tears and jeers,
   And have a good time with you.
   Yes, I'd have a good time with you.
   Refrain

Play Joyfully

Play this part on your recorder when you hear the **B** section.

Dancing in the Rain

The notes of a melody can go up, go down, or stay the same. In what direction do the notes in the red color box go? The green color box?

CD 1–37
MIDI 4

I Don't Care If the Rain Comes Down

Traditional Folk Song from the United States

I don't care if the rain comes down, I'm gon-na dance all day.

I don't care if the rain comes down, I'm gon-na dance all day.

Hey, hey, car-ry me a-way. I'm gon-na dance all day.

Hey, hey, car-ry me a-way. I'm gon-na dance all day.

Move in the Rain

This dance is called a "partner mixer" because you change partners. Try the dance with "I Don't Care If the Rain Comes Down."

Play in the Rain

Play the parts of the song in the color boxes on a xylophone. What other parts of the song can you play using these notes?

Music for the Rain

Listen to the *Raindrop Prelude.* What did the composer do to make this piece sound like rain?

CD 1–41

Raindrop Prelude

by Frédéric Chopin

The *Raindrop Prelude* is one of twenty-four preludes written by Chopin [SHOH-pan]. A prelude, in Chopin's time, was simply a short musical piece.

Look at this small part of the *Raindrop Prelude.* Where is the part that sounds like rain?

MUSIC MAKERS

Frédéric Chopin

Frédéric Chopin (1810–1849) was born in Poland. As a child, he first showed his interest in the piano by asking questions during his older sister's lessons. When his parents realized he was quite talented, they let Chopin have his own piano lessons. Because Chopin was very shy, he enjoyed writing music more than performing. He loved the piano, and wrote almost all of his music—over 200 pieces—for the piano.

Follow the Melody

Follow the listening map as you **listen** to the *Prelude in E Minor*. Find a place where the melody goes up, and where the melody goes down.

by Frédéric Chopin

The *Prelude in E Minor* is also from the twenty-four preludes written by Chopin.

Prelude in E Minor
LISTENING MAP

Take It to the Net Visit *www.sfsuccessnet.com* to find out more about Frédéric Chopin.

Notes to Know

The *Chorus* parts of this African American spiritual use only three notes: *mi, re,* and *do.* **Sing** the pitch syllables for all the parts of the song marked *Chorus.* **Sing** words for the parts marked *Solo.*

CD 1–43
MIDI 5

Oh, Won't You Sit Down

African American Spiritual

Oh, won't you sit down? Lord, I can't sit down.

Oh, won't you sit down? Lord, I can't sit down.

Oh, won't you sit down? Lord, I can't sit down.

'Cause I just got to Heav-en, gon-na look a-round. __

Reading *do re mi*

In this song, *do* is on the second line of the staff. Find *re* and *mi*.

do ___ ___

Which is the lowest pitch?
Which is the highest?

VERSE
Solo

1. Who's   that   yon - der   dressed   in   red? ___

Chorus

Must   be   the   chil - dren   that ___   Mo - ses   led. ___

Solo

Who's   that   yon - der   dressed   in   white? ___

Chorus

D.C. al Fine

Must   be   the   chil - dren   of   the   Is - rael - ite. ___

2.   Who's that yonder dressed in blue?
     Must be the children that are comin' through.
     Who's that yonder dressed in black?
     Must be the hypocrites a-turnin' back.   *Refrain*

Come on Home

Sing "Ida Red" with pitch syllables and hand signs.

Find the five different pitches in the song. What is the last note of the song? Since this song has five different pitches and ends on *do,* we say the song is in *do*-**pentatonic.**

Songs that have only five pitches are sometimes called **pentatonic.**

CD 1–48

Ida Red

Folk Song from Kentucky

Down the road and a-cross the creek, Can't get a let-ter but once a week.

I - da Red,   I - da Blue,   I got stuck on   I - da, too.

Show What You Know!

- Add pitch syllables to these phrases to **create** your own pentatonic song.

- Use the pitches *do, re, mi, so,* and *la.*

- To make the song sound complete, the last pitch must be *do.* End the other phrases on a different pitch.

Sing your compositions or **play** them on a mallet instrument.

How Many Voices?

This song has a verse and a refrain. **Listen** carefully to the voices that sing each part. When do you hear a solo? When do you hear a group?

CD 1–53
MIDI 6

Words by Marilyn Singer

Music by David Eddleman

REFRAIN

This stick here, that stick there.__ Mud, more mud, add mud, good mud.__

This stick here,   that stick there.__ Mud, more mud, add mud, good mud. __

VERSE

1. You   pat.   I   gnaw.   I   pile.   You   store.
2. You guard.   I   pack.   I   dig.   You   stack.
3. I   trim.   You   mold   to   keep   out   cold.

D. C. al Fine

You   pat.   I   gnaw.   I   pile.   You   store.
You guard.   I   pack.   I   dig.   You   stack.
I   trim.   You   mold   to   keep   out   cold.

Name That Voice

Listen to another song with a verse and refrain. Which part is sung by a man? Which part is sung by a group? **Sing** along when the group sings.

CD 1–55
The Hippopotamus Song

by Michael Flanders and Donald Swann

The Hippopotamus Song is part of a show called *At the Drop of a Hat*. The show opened in 1956 and ran for over ten years.

The Hippopotamus Song

by Michael Flanders and Donald Swann

Verse
A bold hippopotamus was standing one day
On the banks of the cool Shalimar.
He gazed at the bottom as it peacefully lay
By the light of the evening star.
Away on the hilltop sat, combing her hair,
His fair hippopotamine maid.
The hippopotamus was no ignoramus
And sang her this sweet serenade.

Refrain
Mud, mud, glorious mud,
Nothing quite like it for cooling the blood.
So follow me, follow, down to the hollow
And there let us wallow in glorious mud.

Michael Flanders and Donald Swann

Michael Flanders (on the right) (1922–1975) and **Donald Swann** (1923–1994) first performed together during their college years in England. Swann was a pianist, and Flanders was an actor. After serving in World War II, they started performing together again. They wrote and sang their songs in musical revues for many years. Their music is always funny and clever.

A Poem to Read with a Friend

Choose a partner to read this poem with you. When the words on the left and the right line up, you read together. When they don't, you read alone. Don't read on the dashes.

Grasshoppers

by Paul Fleischman

Sap's rising	—
—	Ground's warming
Grasshoppers are hatching out	Grasshoppers are hatching out
Autumn-laid eggs	—
—	splitting
Young stepping	—
—	into spring
Grasshoppers hopping high	Grasshoppers hopping —
Grassjumpers jumping —	Grassjumpers jumping far
Vaulting from leaf to leaf	— —
stem to stem plant to plant	leaf to leaf stem to stem
— leapers	Grass leapers
Grass bounders	— bounders
— springers	Grass- springers
Grass soarers	— soarers
Leapfrogging longjumping grasshoppers.	Leapfrogging longjumping grasshoppers.

Alone or Together?

Sometimes you sing alone. Sometimes a musical instrument plays along with your singing.

Listen to two recordings of "Make New Friends." In one, the singers sing alone. In the other, you will hear an **accompaniment.** A string quartet, four string instruments, plays along. The lowest sounding instrument is the cello [CHEHL-oh].

An **accompaniment** is a part that supports a main melody. It is usually played by one or more instruments.

CD 2–1

Make New Friends

Traditional Round

I
E♭

Make new friends, but keep ___ the ___ old, ___

II

One is sil - ver and the oth - er gold.

make

▲ Place right fist over left fist and twist, then repeat.

Sing and Sign Together

Now **sing** the song yourself. Practice signing it as you sing.

new

▲ Right hand sweeps up in an arc.

friends

▲ Lock index fingers together, then reverse and repeat.

Playing Alone

Listen to Yo-Yo Ma play a cello solo without accompaniment.

CD 2–4

Bourrée 1

**from *Suite No. 3 in C Major for Unaccompanied Cello*
by Johann Sebastian Bach**

Bach [bahk] composed a series of pieces for solo cello.

Tune In

"Bach takes you to a very quiet place within yourself, to the inner core, a place where you are calm and at peace."
—Yo-Yo Ma

M·U·S·I·C M·A·K·E·R·S

Yo-Yo Ma

Yo-Yo Ma (born 1955) was born in Paris into a musical family. His father was a violinist. His mother was a singer. He began playing the cello when he was very young. When the Ma family moved to the United States, Yo-Yo's parents enrolled him at the famous Juilliard School of Music in New York City. He was only nine years old at the time.

Ma has played as a soloist with many great orchestras. He also plays recitals and performs with other famous musicians from the fields of jazz and popular music.

Playing with Friends

Now **listen** to Yo-Yo Ma play with an accompaniment. What instrument plays with him?

CD 2–5
Mit Humor

**from *5 Stücke im Volkston*
by Robert Schumann**

Robert Schumann [SHOO-mahn] composed this piece to be accompanied by the piano.

Yo-Yo Ma can also perform as an accompanist. **Listen** to how he accompanies the singing of Bobby McFerrin.

CD 2–6
Musette

by Johann Sebastian Bach

A musette is a dance. It is also a kind of bagpipe. Can you hear the drone-like sound of the bagpipe in the cello part?

Take It to the Net Go to *www.sfsuccessnet.com* to find out more about Yo-Yo Ma and Bobby McFerrin.

Musical Marketplace

In Latin America, outdoor marketplaces, or flea markets, are very colorful. People sell many things there. **Sing** this song about a flea market where musical instruments are sold.

CD 2–7

La pulga de San José

Adapted Spanish words by José-Luis Orozco

Musical arrangement by José-Luis Orozco
Folk Song from Latin America

En la pul - ga de San Jo - sé

yo com - pré u - na gui - ta - rra,

ta - ra, ta - ra, ta - rra, la gui - ta - rra.

Va - ya u - sted, va - ya u - sted

Play in the Market

Play these **ostinatos** as you **sing** this song. Add one part at a time. Choose an instrument you would like to hear with the song.

An **ostinato** is a repeated rhythm or melody pattern.

1.

2.

a la pul - ga de San Jo - sé.

Va - ya u - sted, va - ya u - sted

a la pul - ga de San Jo - sé.

2. *En la pulga de San José,*
   yo compré un clarinete,
   nete, nete, nete, el clarinete,
   tara, tara, tarra, la guitarra. Refrain

3. *En la pulga de San José,*
   yo compré un violín,
   lin, lin, lin, el violín,
   nete, nete, nete, el clarinete,
   tara, tara, tarra, la guitarra. Refrain

Review, Assess,

What Do You Know?

1. Look at the notation of *"Au clair de la lune"* on page 18.

   a. Point to two pitches that show the melody moving up.

   b. Point to two pitches that show the melody moving down.

   c. Point to two pitches that show the melody repeating.

2. Which of these patterns shows AB form?

   a. ● ■ ●   c. ● ■

   b. ● ●   d. ● ■ ▲

What Do You Hear? 1

 CD 2–10

You will hear five musical examples. Point to a place where the melody moves upward, downward, or stays the same.

1.	upward	downward	same
2.	upward	downward	same
3.	upward	downward	same
4.	upward	downward	same
5.	upward	downward	same

Perform, Create

What You Can Do

Sing and Move with Expression

Sing "I Don't Care If the Rain Comes Down" on page 24.

- Sing the first two lines *piano.* Use small steady beat movements as you sing.

- Sing the last two lines *forte.* Use large steady beat movements as you sing.

Perform Rhythmic Ostinatos

Sing "Ding, Dong, Diggidiggidong" on page 14 with the recording. Softly pat one of these three ostinatos as you sing.

Create a Melody

- Create a melody for the poem, "Rain," using , and .

- Use these pitches.

- Teach your friends to sing your melody.

Rain

by Robert Louis Stevenson

The rain is raining all around,
It falls on field and tree,
It rains on the umbrellas here,
And on the ships at sea.

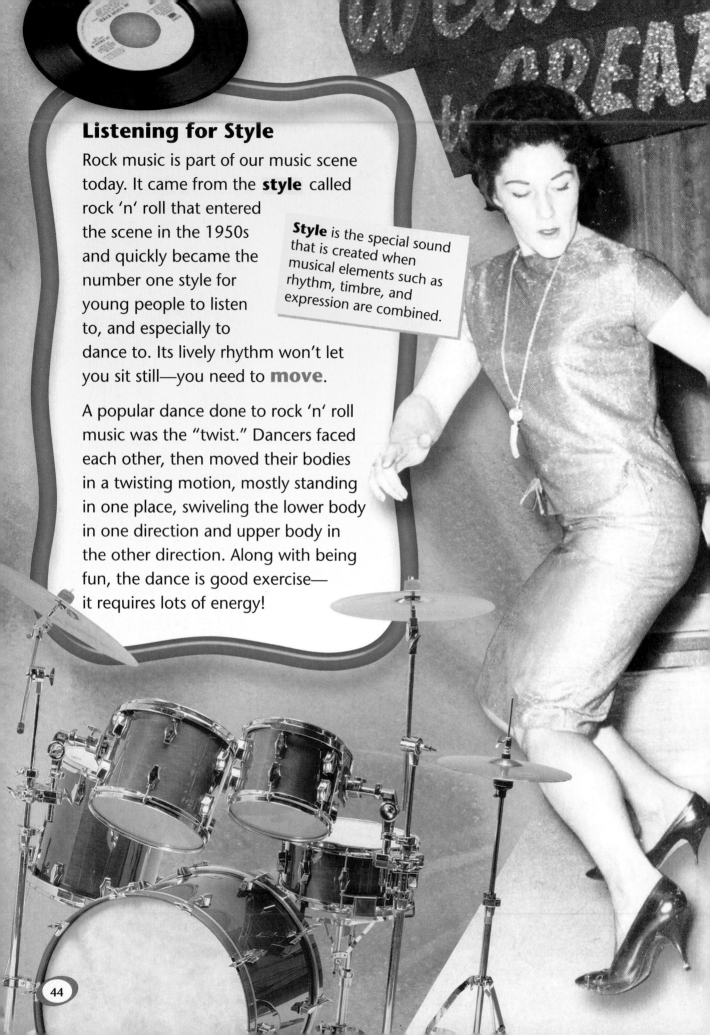

Listening for Style

Rock music is part of our music scene today. It came from the **style** called rock 'n' roll that entered the scene in the 1950s and quickly became the number one style for young people to listen to, and especially to dance to. Its lively rhythm won't let you sit still—you need to **move**.

> **Style** is the special sound that is created when musical elements such as rhythm, timbre, and expression are combined.

A popular dance done to rock 'n' roll music was the "twist." Dancers faced each other, then moved their bodies in a twisting motion, mostly standing in one place, swiveling the lower body in one direction and upper body in the other direction. Along with being fun, the dance is good exercise—it requires lots of energy!

Exploring Music

▲ Chubby Checker, a rock 'n' roll star from the 1960s, doing the "twist."

Dance the Twist

Sing "Peppermint Twist." Then, "twist" along with the song.

CD 2–15

Peppermint Twist

Words and Music by Henry Glover and Joey Dee

They got a new dance and it goes like this. _
Meet _ me, pal, down on forty-fifth street. _

The name of the dance is the Pep-per-mint Twist. _
Where the _ Pepper-mint _ Twist - ers meet, _

Well, you'll like _____ it like this, _ the Pep-per-mint Twist.
And you'll learn _____ to do this, _ the Pep-per-mint Twist.

Well, 'round and 'round, up and down,

'round and 'round, up and down, 'round and 'round and up and down,

one two three kick, one two three jump.

Well, al - right __ all night, __ well, al-right.
It's o - kay __ all day, __ it's o - kay.

And you'll learn _____ to do this, __ the Pep-per-mint Twist.

Hey! _____ Hey! _____

And you'll learn _____ to do this, __ the Pep-per-mint Twist!

TRAIN TO FREEDOM

Many African American spirituals were used to send messages along the Underground Railroad. What message does this song send? **Listen** to "Train Is A-Comin'." **Sing** the song and learn all the verses.

CD 2–17
MIDI 7

Train Is A-Comin'

African American Spiritual

1. Train is a - com - in', oh, yes,
2. Better get your tick - et, oh, yes,

Train is a - com - in', ___ oh, yes,
Better get your tick - et, ___ oh, yes,

Get on Board!

Play these ostinatos with the song.

On the first verse, use the cabasa. On the second verse, add the vibraslap. On the third verse, you can add the drum.

Train is a-com-in', train is a-com-in',
Better get your tick - et, better get your tick - et,

Train is a-com-in', oh, yes.
Better get your tick - et, oh, yes.

3. Room for many others, oh, yes,
   Room for many others, oh, yes,
   Room for many others, room for many others,
   Room for many others, oh, yes.

Fast or Slow—Go, Beat, Go!

Have you ever thought about how different songs go at different speeds? In music, we call this the **tempo** of a song.

Here are some words musicians use for tempo.

> **Tempo** is the speed of the beat.

adagio	= slow
moderato	= medium
allegro	= fast
accelerando	= getting faster
ritardando	= getting slower

M·U·S·I·C M·A·K·E·R·S

Joseph Joubert

Joseph Joubert [zhoo-BARE] (born 1958) is a pianist, composer, arranger, and accompanist. He began piano lessons at age eight. At the young age of sixteen, he performed in New York City with full orchestra. He accompanied singer Kathleen Battle in recital at the White House for the American and Russian presidents in 1994. His musical arrangements in this book include "Hush, Hush," "Children, Go Where I Send Thee," and "Little Johnny Brown." Joubert lives in New Jersey.

CD 2–19
Interview with Joseph Joubert

Same Song, But Different

Choo-Choo Joubert is based on "Train Is A-Comin'."
Listen for the different tempos in the song as you follow the listening map.

CD 2–20

Choo-Choo Joubert

by Joseph Joubert

The form of this piece is theme and variation. How many different ways does the composer use the melody?

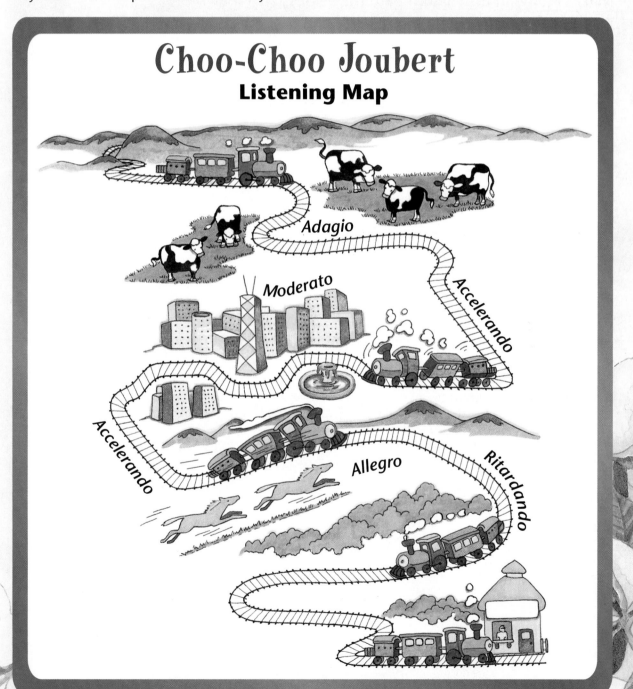

Choo-Choo Joubert
Listening Map

Adagio

Moderato

Accelerando

Accelerando

Allegro

Ritardando

SNEAKY SNAKE RHYTHM

Some snakes like to hide in tall grass. These snakes like to hide in rhythms. Find the snakes hiding in the rhythm patterns below. Each snake ties two notes together.

Tune In

Snakes have no eyelids, so they can't blink. They also can't hear, so a rattlesnake doesn't hear its own rattle!

Tie It Together!

The song below is written with **ties** instead of snakes. **Read** the rhythm of "Black Snake."

> A **tie** is a musical symbol that joins two notes together to create a longer sound.

CD 2–21

Black Snake

Traditional

Black snake, black snake, where are ___ you hid - ing?

Black snake, black snake, where are ___ you hid - ing?

Black snake, black snake, where are ___ you hid - ing?

Don't you bite _____ me! _____

Two Beats, Three Sounds

The highlighted measure has the new rhythm pattern with three sounds. Which sound is the longest?

Name the New Rhythm

"Mister Ram Goat-O" is a song from Trinidad. In Caribbean songs, animals are sometimes called Mister, brother, or some other title of respect.

Listen to the recording of "Mister Ram Goat-O" and **sing** and clap on the word *Bam-ban-dy-a.*

CD 2–26

Mister Ram Goat-O

Folk Song from Trinidad

Call
Mis - ter Ram Goat - O! Bam - ban - dy - a.

Call
Mis - ter Ram Goat - O! Bam - ban - dy - a.

Call
Can you lend me a ra - zor? Bam - ban - dy - a.

Call
It's to shave off my long beard. Bam - ban - dy - a.

Musical Homonyms

There are different ways to **write** rhythms that sound the same.

This pattern can also be written like this:

The new rhythm can also be written like this:

What rhythm do you know that sounds the same as ?

The new rhythm pattern can also be written like this:

This rhythm pattern is called **syncopation**.

Syncopation is rhythm in which the note that is stressed comes between two beats.

Find the syncopation in "Mister Ram Goat-O." Then **sing** the song and clap the syncopated patterns.

Now Hear the Rhythm

This song is about *Carnaval*, a festival celebrated in many Spanish-speaking countries. Look at the notation. How many syncopated rhythms do you find? **Sing** the song.

CD 2–31

Ahora voy a cantarles

English Words by Alice Firgau   **(Now Hear the Song)**   *Folk Song from Argentina*

1. Aho - ra voy a can - tar - les
1. Now hear the song I'll sing you

has - ta que_a - pun - te_el lu - ce - ro.
Un - til the dawn is _____ break - ing.

56

Show What You Know!

Clap and say these patterns with rhythm syllables. Then **play** them on percussion instruments with "Ahora voy a cantarles."

Los car - na - va - les ya vie - nen
All through the night hap - py peo - ple

des - de la ci - ma del ce - rro.
Come down from on the ____ moun - tain.

2. ¡Todos, toditos, arriba!
   ¡El carnaval ha llegado!
   Domingo, lunes y martes,
   tres días y se acabó.

2. Come on, my friends, come join me.
   Carnaval time is here now,
   Sunday and Monday and Tuesday,
   Three days, no more 'til next year.

FOLLOW THE LEADER

"Great Day" is a **call-and-response** song. **Listen** to the song and clap the responses.

Then clap the calls and **sing** the responses. Use dynamics!

> **Call and response** is a form of choral singing. The call is sung by a leader and the response is usually sung by a group.

CD 2–35

GREAT DAY

African American Spiritual

REFRAIN

Great ___ day!   Great   day,   the right-eous march-in'.

Great ___ day!   God's gon-na build up   Zi - on's walls.   *Fine*

VERSE *Call*

1. The   char - iot   rode   on   the   moun - tain   top. ___
2. This   is   the   day   of ___   ju - bi - lee. ___

58

Call to Move!

Move to this pattern on the response phrases in "Great Day."

God's gonna   build up   Zion's   walls

Response

God's gon - na build up Zi - on's walls.
God's gon - na build up Zi - on's walls.

Call

My God he spoke and the char - iot stopped.
The Lord has set his ___ peo - ple free. ___

Response

D. C. al Fine

God's gon - na build up Zi - on's walls.
God's gon - na build up Zi - on's walls.

"John Kanaka" is a work song. It has been sung by dockworkers in California to keep rhythm while they load cargo.

Listen to "John Kanaka." Can you hear a repeating phrase?

CD 2–37

John Kanaka

Sea Shanty

I heard, I heard the old man say,

John Ka - na - ka, na - ka, too - lai - ay.

To - day, to - day is a hol - i - day,

See the Question

In music, a phrase is like a musical sentence. Some phrases ask musical questions. Other phrases give musical answers.

Sing the first phrase of "John Kanaka" using pitch syllables. On what pitch does the phrase end? Does it sound finished? This is the question phrase.

Find the Answer

Now **sing** the second phrase of the song, using pitch syllables. On what pitch does this phrase end? An answer phrase often ends on *do.*

Identify the question and answer phrases in "John Kanaka." Some of your class can sing the question phrases, while others sing the answer phrases. **Play** the question and answer rhythms on recorders using the pitch "A."

John   Ka - na - ka,   na - ka,   too - lai - ay.

Too - lai - ay,   oh,   too - lai - ay,

John   Ka - na - ka,   na - ka,   too - lai - ay.

Play with Me

Play an accompaniment to "John Kanaka." Some of your classmates can sing the song, while the others play.

Dance with Me

Now try these dance steps to "John Kanaka."

Lines 1 and 3:
Do a slide-close. ▶

◀ Lines 2, 4, and 6: Do a clapping pattern.

Line 5: Do a
right-arm swing. ▶

Listen to the Dance

Bransle de la Torche has twelve question phrases and twelve answer phrases.

CD 2–39

Bransle de la Torche

**from *Dances from Terpsichore*
by Michael Praetorius**

Michael Praetorius wrote this piece in 1612.

Step This Way

When you move, sometimes you take big steps. Sometimes you take little steps. You can skip or step in place. A melody also moves. It can move in small steps, skips, or stay in one place.

Sing this famous dance song from the pop music of the 1960s. You may already know it!

CD 2–40

The Loco-Motion

Words and Music by Gerry Goffin and Carole King

A   E♭   Cm

Ev - 'ry - bo - dy's do - in' a brand - new dance __ now,
Move a - round the floor __ in a lo - co - mo - tion,

E♭   Cm

Come on, ba - by, do ___ the lo - co - mo - tion. I
Come on, ba - by, do ___ the lo - co - mo - tion.

E♭   Cm

know you'll get to like it if you give it a chance __ now,
Do it hold - in' hands __ if ___ you get the no - tion,

E♭   Cm

Come on, ba - by, do ___ the lo - co - mo - tion.
Come on, ba - by, do ___ the lo - co - mo - tion.

Melody Moves

Can you find these steps, skips, and repeated pitches in "The Loco-Motion"?

◀ step

◀ skip

◀ repeat

You've got the knack!

My lit-tle ba-by sis-ter can do it with ease, _ It's
There's nev-er been a dance _ that's so eas-y to do, __ It

eas-i-er than learn-in' your A B C's. __ So
e-ven makes you hap-py when you're feel-in' blue. _ So

come on, come on, do ____ the lo-co-mo-tion with me. _
come on, come on, do ____ the lo-co-mo-tion with me.

You got-ta swing your hips now, _ Come on, ba-by, Jump up,

jump back, Oh, well, I think you got the knack. __

Do the Loco-Motion!

Now it's time to learn the dance steps to "The Loco-Motion."
As you **move**, make a chugging motion with your arms.

Everybody's doing a brand-new dance now,

Come on, baby, do the locomotion.

Beautiful Music

Listen to another song written by Carole King.

CD 2–42

Beautiful

written and performed by Carole King

Beautiful is one of the most famous songs from Carole King's album *Tapestry*.

MUSIC MAKERS

CAROLE KING

Carole King (born 1942) has had a career in music since the 1950s. Her first songs were ready to be published while she was just a teenager. With Gerry Goffin, she wrote many popular songs, including "The Loco-Motion." She has also written and recorded her music on her own. One of her albums, *Tapestry,* sold millions of copies.

Morning Melodies

"One Morning Soon" is an African American spiritual, a religious folk song. All the pitch syllables you know are in this song, plus a new note!

Sing the first three measures of the song with pitch syllables and hand signs. Here's a hint: The song starts on *do*.

CD 2–43

One Morning Soon

African American Spiritual

1. One morn - in' soon, ___ one morn - in' soon, ___
2. Down on my knees, ___ down on my knees, ___
3. One day 'bout noon, ___ one day 'bout noon, ___

One morn - in' soon, I heard the an - gels sing - in'.
Down on my knees, I heard the an - gels sing - in'.
One day 'bout noon, I heard the an - gels sing - in'.

Skip Down to a New Note

Now **sing** the last measure of the song with words and **listen** for a new note. Does the note sound higher or lower than *do?* Find the new note in the song.

Since the new note is a skip below *do,* where will the new note go on each of the staffs below?

1.
do ? do

2.
do ? do

3.
do ? do

On This Day

by M. B. Goffstein

On this day
I'm going to pick
a big bouquet
and put it in my shoe
and let it sail away.
And when it gets
across the sea,
how amazed the children
there
will be.

Name the New Note

The new note that is a skip below *do* is *low la.*

Play this pattern on a bass xylophone.

Then **create** an ostinato to play as a **B** section for "One Morning Soon." Use the pitches above.

Find the New Note

"*Hosisipa*" is a Sioux hand game song. **Listen** to the recording, and then **sing** the song.

CD 2–48

Hosisipa

Native American Game Song of the Sioux

Ho - si - si - pa, ho - si - si - pa, ho - si - si - pa, ho - si.

Arts Connection

This doll and cradle board were made by the Dakota Sioux in the 1800s.

Sign the New Note

In *"Hosisipa,"* *do* is on the second line. On what note does the song end? **Sing** *"Hosisipa"* with pitch syllables and hand signs.

mi   re   do   low la

Show What You Know!

Sing each example with pitch syllables and hand signs. Then **play** them on resonator bells.

Exploring

Everyone has a family tree. Mother, brothers, aunts, and cousins are all part of your family tree. **Sing** "Family Tree." What family members does the singer include in his story?

CD 2–53

Family Tree

Words and Music by John Forster and Tom Chapin

VERSE

F   C

1. Be - fore the days of Jell - O   lived a pre - his - tor - ic fel - low
2. My grand-pa came from Rus-sia;   my grand-ma came from Prus-sia;
3. One fine day I may go   to Tie - rra del Fue-go.

C   F

Who loved a maid and court-ed her be - neath the ban - yan tree.
They met in No - va Sco - tia, had my dad in Ten - nes - see.
Per - haps I'll meet my wife there and we'll move to Tim - buk - tu.

F   C

And they had lots of chil-dren and their chil - dren all had chil-dren.
Then they moved to Yo-ko - ha - ma, where Dad - dy met my ma - ma.
And our kid will be bi-ling-ual, and though she may stay sin - gle,

C   C   F

And they kept on hav - ing chil-dren un - til one of them had me.
Her dad's from Al - a - bam - a and her mom's part Cher - o - kee.
She could, of course, go min-gle with the king of Kat-man-du.

Listen for a Special Sound

Each time you hear a new voice in this song, you hear a different vocal **timbre.** How many different timbres do you hear?

Timbre is the special sound each voice or instrument makes.

A Family 'Round the World

Some of the places listed here are named in "Family Tree." Speak each one.

Create a word chain using these place names. Combine two or more and speak them in rhythm. Try this!

Yokohama   Alabama
Madagascar   Tierra del Fuego
Russia   Alaska
Nova Scotia   Timbuktu
Tennessee

Yo - ko - ha - ma, Ma - da - gas - car, A - la - ba - ma, Tim - buk - tu.

Find Your Place in the World

The stars on the map show some of the places named above. Can you match a name to each star?

Take It to the Net Go to *www.sfsuccessnet.com* to find out more about Tom Chapin and his music.

74

MUSIC MAKERS

Tom Chapin

Tom Chapin (born 1945) is a gifted singer, guitar player, and songwriter who loves doing good things for others.

Chapin has given many concerts and made many recordings. He helps groups such as *Save the Children*. He wrote a collection of songs called *Sing a Whale Song* to help save endangered whales. He lives with his family in New York State.

Singing an ECHO

Have you ever called into a large, empty space and heard your voice echo back? Here's an echo song you can **sing** with your classmates.

CD 3-1

I'm on My Way

African American Spiritual

1. I'm on my way (I'm on my way) to the free-dom land, (to the free-dom

land,) I'm on my way (I'm on my way) to the free-dom land, (to the free-dom

land,) I'm on my way (I'm on my way) to the free-dom land, (to the free-dom

land,) I'm on my way, — thank God, I'm on my way. _____

2. I asked my friends . . . to go with me, . . . *(3 times)*
   I'm on my way, thank God, I'm on my way.

3. If they won't come . . . then I'll go alone, . . . *(3 times)*
   I'm on my way, thank God, I'm on my way.

4. I'm on my way . . . and I won't turn back, . . . *(3 times)*
   I'm on my way, thank God, I'm on my way.

Singing an Echo

"Old Texas" is also an echo song. Pat the beat on your knees and **sing** the melody as an echo after the teacher. Notice that when a long note is held in the melody, the echo creates a thicker texture.

Sing "Old Texas" in groups. One group sings the melody while the other group sings the echo.

CD 3–3

Old Texas

Cowboy Song from Oklahoma

1. I'm goin' to leave _____ old __ Tex - as now, (echo)
2. They've plowed and fenced _____ my __ cat - tle range, (echo)
3. I'll take my horse, _____ I'll __ take my rope,

They've got no use _____ for the long - horn cow. (echo)
And the peo - ple there _____ are __ all so strange. (echo)
And hit the trail _____ up - on a lope.

4. Say *adiós* to the Alamo
And turn my head t'ward Mexico.

Sounds on the Trail

Listen to this piece by Ferde Grofé.

CD 3–5
On the Trail

from *Grand Canyon Suite* by Ferde Grofé

Ferde Grofé wrote this piece after he traveled through the Grand Canyon.

Blankets of Sound

Sing this Slovakian lullaby. What words in this song suggest going to sleep?

 CD 3–6
MIDI 8

Hej pada pada
(Dewdrops)

English Words by Ellen K. Traeger

Lullaby from Slovakia

Hej pa - da pa - da ro - sič - ka,
Dew - drops a - fall - ing from the skies,

Spa - ly by mo - je o - čič - ka.
Drow - sy and sleep - y, close your eyes.

Spa - ly by mo - je, Spa - ly by aj tvo - je,
Drow - sy and sleep - y, go to sleep my ba - by.

Spa - ly by du - ša mo - ja o - bo - je.
Dream of the dew - drops fall - ing from the skies.

Layer the Sound

Sing *"Hej pada pada"* without accompaniment. Now **sing** it again with accompaniment. Every time you add another voice, or another instrument, you create a thicker **texture.**

> **Texture** is how thin or thick music sounds. It is created by layering sounds on top of one another.

Playing with Texture

Play an accompaniment for the song on instruments. What instruments would you add to create a thicker texture?

More Slovakian Music

Listen to this piece by Leoš Janáček.

CD 3–10

Kalamajka

**from *Moravian Dances*
by Leoš Janáček**

Moravia is part of the Czech Republic. Dance is an important part of Moravian life.

Review, Assess,

What Do You Know?

1. Match the musical terms with the correct definitions.

   a. *adagio*   • speed of the beat
   b. *allegro*   • slow
   c. tempo   • moderate (medium)
   d. *moderato*   • fast

2. Look at these patterns. Decide if each one is moving by step, skip, or repeated tone.

   a.   **c.**   **e.**

   b.   **d.**

What Do You Hear? 2

 CD 3–11

Listen to four musical examples.
Point to the word that best
describes the tempo of each example.

1. *accelerando*   *ritardando*
2. *allegro*   *adagio*
3. *allegro*   *adagio*
4. *accelerando*   *ritardando*

Perform, Create

What You Can Do

Sing an Echo

Sing "I'm on My Way" on page 76 with half the class singing the first part and the other half singing the echo. Be sure to hold, or sustain, the long notes.

Perform Call and Response

Perform this call-and-response speech piece with your classmates.

Call .... *Response*

Corn flakes, oat - meal, ap-ple crisp, You can't go wrong.

Call .... *Response*

Tur - nips, broc-co - li, rut-a-bag-a, peas, Make me grow strong!

Create a Melody

Turn the speech piece into a song! Create a melody for your call-and-response piece. Use these pitches.

E G A B D E

Get on the Band Wagon

Different musical groups play different kinds of music. How many different kinds of music can you name?

Listen to these different types of bands. How will you **move** to each of these pieces? Match the photographs to the music you hear.

CD 3–15
American Band Montage

Learning the Language of MUSIC

Move to the Music

"Let's Get the Rhythm of the Band"
is made for dancing! **Move** the way the
words suggest as you **sing** the song.

CD 3–16

Let's Get the Rhythm of the Band

Based on a Children's Rhyme

New Words and Music by Cheryl Warren Mattox

Let's get the rhy-thm of the band, oh yeah, _

We got the rhy-thm of the band. _____

Let's get the rhy-thm of the hand, clap your hands now,
snap your fin - gers,
wave your hands high,

We got the rhy-thm of the hand. _____

Let's get the rhy-thm of the feet, stomp it out with me,
jump up high __ now,
march in time __ now,

We got   the   rhy - thm   of   the   feet, _____

Let's   get   the   rhy - thm   of   the   band.

Let's   get   the   rhy - thm   of   the   band.

Hops and Glides

Listen to *"El gallo pinto"* as it is sung in Spanish. What do you notice about the beginnings of the words in the last line? Have fun with the Spanish words as you learn to **sing** this song.

CD 3–18
MIDI 9

El gallo pinto
(The Painted Rooster)

English Words by Jorge Winston-La Paz　　　　*Spanish Words and Music by Tita Maya*

El ga - llo pin - to no pin - ta,
The paint - ed roos - ter's no paint - er,

El que pin - ta es el pin - tor;
For the paint - er's the one who paints;

Que al ga - llo pin - to las pin - tas
The one who paint - ed that roos - ter

Pin - ta por pin - ta pin - tó.
Paint - ed each feath - er so quaint.

Smooth or Separated?

Listen again to the recording of *"El gallo pinto."*
You will hear the strings play *legato* and the
trumpets play *staccato*.

Legato means "smooth and connected."

Staccato means "short and separated."

Move to the Music

How would you **move** to this song? **Create** a dance
for *legato* and *staccato* movements. You might use the
movements shown below.

 MIDI Experiment with *legato* and *staccato* sounds
in the accompaniment of *"El gallo pinto."*

The Long and Short of It

You can hear *staccato* and *legato* sounds in this piece.
Listen to the music and follow the listening map.
It shows the first two phrases of each section.

CD 3–22
Gavotte

by François-Joseph Gossec

Gossec originally wrote this piece as a violin lesson for his
students. It is performed here by flute and orchestra.

Gavotte
LISTENING MAP

Styles in Art

Legato and *staccato* are words used to describe musical sounds that are smooth or separated. You can *see* smooth and separated in art, too. These two paintings are examples of two different styles. The first one shows a fluid, or smooth, line. The second uses a technique called pointillism, where the painter actually makes the entire picture out of dots of color.

Arts Connection

The Whirl
by Frantisek Kupka
(1871–1957) ▶

Arts Connection

Sous les Pins a Carqueiranne
by Louis Gaidan (1847–1925) ▼

▼ Close-up

Market Rhythms

Kingston is the capital city of Jamaica. "Kingston Market" tells about an outdoor market where many people shop.

Listen to the song to find the syncopated rhythm patterns.

Kingston Market

Words and Music by Irving Burgie

CD 3–23

Have you ev - er seen a rain - bow or a

gar - den bloom - ing bright? Heard the

shuf - fle of a thou - sand feet or

drums from morn - ing 'til night?

90

Jamaican Rhythm

In Jamaica, many groups of drummers play on the streets. **Play** this accompaniment on drums as you **sing** the song.

VERSE

REFRAIN

REFRAIN

Come we   go down,   come we   go down,

come   we   go   down   to   King - ston   Mar - ket.

Come we   go down,   come we   go down,

down   to   King - ston   Mar - ket.

Chicken 'n' Rhythm

"Chicken on the Fence Post" is a song with silly words.
Sing the song and **move** to the music.

CD 3–25

Chicken on the Fence Post

Play-Party Song from the United States

1. Chick-en on the fence post, can't dance Jo-sey,

Chick-en on the fence post, can't dance Jo-sey,

Clap Like a Chicken

Use rhythm syllables to say and clap the rhythm of the song. Which lines of rhythm are the same?

Chickens Composing!

Compose your own rhythm piece using ♩, ♫, and ♬. Use the same rhythm pattern for three lines of the piece, and a different rhythm for the fourth line. **Perform** your composition while the class sings the song.

Chick - en on the fence post, can't dance Jo - sey,

Hel - lo, Su - san Brown - y - o.

2. Choose my partner and come dance Josey, . . .

3. Chew my gum while I dance Josey, . . .

4. Shoestring's broke and I can't dance Josey, . . .

5. Hold my mule while I dance Josey, . . .

6. Hair in the butter, can't dance Josey, . . .

7. Briar in my heels, can't dance Josey, . . .

8. Stumped my toe, can't dance Josey, . . .

Love Those Rhythms!

Listen to "Love Somebody" and raise your hand when you hear . Find the in the notation below. Then **read** and **perform** the rhythm.

Love Somebody

CD 3–31

Folk Song from the United States

Love some-bod - y, yes, I do, Love some-bod - y, yes, I do,

Love some-bod - y, yes, I do, Love some-bod-y but I won't tell who!

More Rhythms to Love

Read and **perform** this pattern. How many lines of rhythm are the same?

Clap the entire pattern again as you **sing** "Love Somebody." Do the rhythms and the song end at the same time?

Did you know that Valentine's Day has been celebrated for 1,500 years?

Show What You Know!

Create your own four-beat rhythmic ostinato, using any of the rhythms below. **Play** your ostinato on percussion instruments as you **sing** "Love Somebody."

Which of the following rhythms last for one beat? Which rhythms last for two beats?

Songs of the Old West

"Old Dan Tucker" is an American frontier song.

Sing "Old Dan Tucker." **Listen** for two different sections of the song. What makes them different?

Old Dan Tucker

CD 3–36
MIDI 10

Folk Song from the United States

Ⓐ **VERSE**

1. Old Dan Tuck-er was a might-y man, He

washed his face in the fry - ing pan,

Combed his hair with a wag - on wheel,

Had a tooth - ache in his heel;

A Two-Part Party Song

Look for the letters **A** and **B** in the song. A song that has two different sections is called two-part, or **A B**, form. In this song, the two sections are marked **verse** and **refrain.**

The **verse** of a song is a section where the melody stays the same even when the lyrics change.

The **refrain** of a song is sung the same way every time it repeats.

REFRAIN

B

F
So get out the way, Old Dan Tuck - er;

C₇   F
Get out the way, Old Dan Tuck - er;

F
Get out the way, Old Dan Tuck - er,

C₇   F
You're too late to get your sup - per.

2. Old Dan Tucker came to town,
   Riding a billy goat, leading a hound;
   Hound dog barked, then billy goat jumped;
   Dan fell off and landed on a stump;   *Refrain*

Time to Play

With a partner, create ways to show Ⓐ Ⓑ form.
Here are a few ideas.

- **Move** a different way for each section.

- **Sing** the song and make the Ⓑ section louder
  or softer.

- **Play** this accompaniment during the verse.
  Then **create** your own part for the refrain.

Music for Dancing

Flop-Eared Mule is a dance tune from the Old West. Dance tunes were also known as "fiddle tunes" because they were created and played by violin players, known as fiddlers. **Listen** to discover the form of the piece.

CD 3–39

Flop-Eared Mule

Traditional American as performed by Don Wiles, Jim Widner, and Vivian Williams

This fiddle tune is over 100 years old.

Long ago, settlers held dances so people could get to know one another. The fiddle was the most popular instrument at dances.

Crocodile Form

Listen to this funny song from the musical film *Peter Pan.*

CD 3–40

Words by Jack Lawrence

Never Smile at a Crocodile

Music by Frank Churchill

Nev - er smile at a croc - o - dile, No, you

can't get friend - ly with a croc - o - dile, Don't be

tak - en in by his wel - come grin, He's im -

ag - in - ing how well you'd fit with - in his skin.

Nev - er smile at a croc - o - dile, Nev - er

tip your hat and stop to talk a while. 1.,2. Nev - er

3. Don't be

Beware of Crocodile Moves!

Look at the **A** and **B** sections as you sing this song. Watch out for the **_D.C. al Fine_** at the end of the **B** section. Where will you go next?

D.C. al Fine is an Italian musical term that tells you to go back to the beginning of the song and sing until you see the word Fine [FEE-neh].

Make up a clapping game with a friend. Play it as you sing the song. Move to a new partner for each section.

run, walk a - way, say "Good-night," not "Good day!" Clear the
rude, nev - er mock, throw a kiss, not a rock. Clear the

aisle and nev - er smile at Mis - ter Croc - o - dile.
aisle and nev - er smile at Mis - ter Croc - o - dile.

B You may ve - ry well be well - bred,

Lots of et - i - quette in your head,

But there's al - ways some spe - cial case, time or

place to for - get et - i - quette.

Sing a Lullaby

This is a very old, well-known lullaby from Taiwan. Use the recorded Pronunciation Practice to learn to **sing** the song in Mandarin. Then **sing** it again in English.

 CD 4–1

Hwa yuan li-de young wa wa
(Garden Lullaby)

Words by Po-Yang Chou
English Words by Ellen Williams

Music by Chuen-Taur Su

妹 妹 背 著 洋 娃 娃　 走 到 花 園 来 看 花
Mai mai bay ge young wa wa　jou dau hwa yuan lai kan hwa
Lit - tle sis - ter with her doll　Walks a-mong the gar - den walls.

娃 娃 哭 了 叫 媽 媽　 樹 上 小 鳥 笑 哈 哈
wa wa koo le jau ma ma　shu shan siau niau siau ha ha.
"Ma - ma," cries the ba - by doll.　From the trees birds sing their calls.

Find the New Pitch

"*Hwa yuan li-de young wa wa*" contains these pitches that you can already **read.**

Listen to the song again. On which pitch does the song start? Find the place in the song where you hear a new pitch. Is it higher or lower than the pitches you already know?

Take a Step Down

The new pitch is even lower than *low la.* It is a step below *low la.*

Music of Taiwan

Listen to this piece for solo piano. The melody repeats several times.

CD 4–8
Lantern Festival

**from *Taiwan Suite*
by Ma Shui-Long**

Lantern Festival is about the celebration on the fifteenth day of the Chinese New Year.

Tune In

The piano has been played in Taiwan for more than 100 years. Many Taiwanese children study piano.

M·U·S·I·C M·A·K·E·R·S

Ma Shui-Long

Ma Shui-Long (born 1939) is a well-known composer in Taiwan. He mixes traditional Taiwanese folk songs into his compositions. He writes music for orchestra, chamber ensemble, piano solo, vocal solo, and chorus. Ma has received many awards for his work. *Lantern Festival* is part of a collection of his piano pieces.

Arts Connection

The Beloved Grandchildren by Li Mei-Shu. This painting shows the artist's grandchildren in the mid-1900s. ▼

Meet the Artist

Li Mei-Shu (1902–1983) was interested in music and painting from the time he was a child in Taiwan. While going to school, he taught himself to paint in his spare time. He later studied painting in Japan, then returned to Taiwan to teach. Li especially liked painting pictures of people. His favorite subject was the Chinese people.

Take It to the Net Visit *www.sfsuccessnet.com* to learn more about Chinese and Taiwanese music styles.

New Note Coming Through

There's a new pitch you can learn in this folk song from Alabama. **Listen** for the new pitch in the recording. Notice that the song starts on *do.*

CD 4–9
MIDI 11

Alabama Gal

Folk Song from Alabama

1. Come through 'na hur - ry,
2. I don't know how, how,

Come through 'na hur - ry,
I don't know how, how,

Come through 'na hur - ry,
I don't know how, how,

Al - a - bam - a Gal.
Al - a - bam - a Gal.

3. I showed you how, how, *(3 times)*
Alabama Gal.

4. Ain't I rock candy, *(3 times)*
Alabama Gal.

What's the Pitch Name?

The pitch that is a step lower than *low la* is called *low so*.
You already know a hand sign for *so*. Can you guess
what the hand sign is for *low so*?

Find the *low so* highlighted in the song. Then **sing**
"Alabama Gal" with pitch syllables and hand signs.

Play-Party Time

Now it's time to learn the play-party, or dance, that
goes with "Alabama Gal." **Move** like the children
pictured below.

GET UP AND SING!

Children in the city often sing "Old Man Mosie" as they jump rope. **Sing** "Old Man Mosie." On what words do you sing *mi-re-do*? Where is the syncopation? Where is the tie?

CD 4–15

OLD MAN MOSIE

Singing Game from the United States

Swing style

Old man Mo - sie, sick in the bed,

Called the doc - tor, the doc - tor said,

"Please step for - ward, turn a - round, —

Do the ho - key po - key, and get out of town."

Get Up and Read!

Read this ostinato using pitch syllables and hand signs. Then **sing** the ostinato with "Old Man Mosie."

do

Advice to Small Children
by Edward Anthony

Eat no green apples, or you'll droop,
Be careful not to get the croup,
Avoid the chicken-pox and such,
And don't fall out of windows much.

Show What You Know!

Sing this ostinato using pitch syllables and hand signs. Try it in two groups. Half of the class will sing the ostinato while the other half sings "Alabama Gal," on page 106.

do

Play the pitches of the ostinato on a xylophone while the rest of the class sings "Alabama Gal."

Welcome to the String Family

String instruments make sounds through vibration. The strings must be stretched across an open space, such as a box. The box amplifies, or makes louder, the sounds made by the vibrating string.

Try this experiment.

◀ Stretch a rubber band across the top of a box.

Pluck the rubber band to make it vibrate. ▶

How else could you make the rubber band vibrate?

Ways to Play

Here are two ways to play a string instrument.
Each way causes a string to vibrate.

◄ Plucking a string is like snapping the rubber band over the box.

◄ When bowing [BOH-ing], the player moves a bow across the strings.

 Video Library Learn more about string instruments from around the world in *String Instruments: Bowed* and *String Instruments: Plucked.*

Meet the Players

Four string instruments have become a regular part of a large musical group called an orchestra. They are the violin, the viola, the cello [CHEHL-oh], and the string bass [base].

What do you see about these instruments that is the same? What do you see that is different? Which instrument do you think plays the lowest sounds? Why?

Cello▶

◀String bass

String Tunes

Listen to this recording of a famous French melody.

- Hear the piece in **unison.**
- Hear the strings play **arco,** in a round.
- Hear the strings play **pizzicato,** on different parts.

Unison means that all instruments play the same notes.

Arco means "bowed."

Pizzicato means "plucked."

 CD 4–17
Frère Jacques

**Traditional French
arranged by Buryl Red**

This melody has been sung around the world in many different languages.

Listen to *Winter*. Do you hear bowed or plucked strings?

Violin ▶

CD 4–18
Winter, Movement 2

**from *the Four Seasons*
by Antonio Vivaldi**

The four sections of this piece for string orchestra match the four seasons of the year.

Describe the sounds you hear in this string quartet.

CD 4–19
Movement 4

**from *String Quartet No. 5*
by Béla Bartók**

The players use *pizzicato* and *arco* playing in this piece.

▼ Viola

SING GOOD MORNING!

Listen to "Had to Get Up This Mornin' Soon."
Then **sing** the song and snap your fingers to the
steady beat.

CD 4–20

HAD TO GET UP THIS MORNIN' SOON

African American Song

Had to get up this morn - in' soon,

Had to get up this morn - in' soon,

Had to get up this morn - in' soon, soon,

Had to get up this morn - in' soon.

Morning Harmony

You have already played rhythmic ostinatos. Now you can learn a **melodic ostinato.** A melodic ostinato can be either sung or played on a pitched instrument.

A melody pattern that repeats several times is called a **melodic ostinato.**

Sing this melodic ostinato while the rest of the class sings the **A** section.

Up this morn - in' soon.

Did you know that any time after midnight is actually morning?

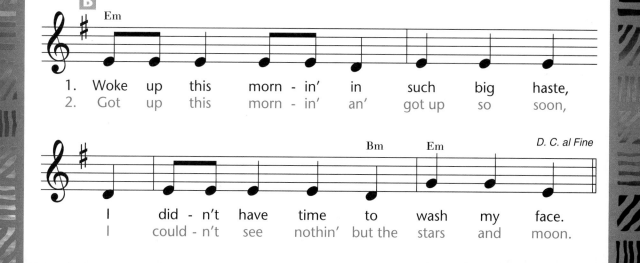

1. Woke up this morn - in' in such big haste,
2. Got up this morn - in' an' got up so soon,

I did - n't have time to wash my face.
I could - n't see nothin' but the stars and moon.

Gathering Harmony

This song is sung in the musical play *Peter Pan* as the children are preparing for bed. What do you call this kind of song? **Listen** to "Tender Shepherd," and then **sing** the song.

CD 4–22

Tender Shepherd

Words by Carolyn Leigh

Music by Mark Charlap

1. Ten - der shep - herd, ten - der shep - herd,
2. Ten - der shep - herd, ten - der shep - herd,

Watch - es o - ver all his sheep.
You for - got to count your sheep,

One, say your pray'rs, and two, close your eyes, And
One in the mead - ow, two in the gar - den,

three, safe and hap - pi - ly fall a - sleep.
Three in the nur - ser - y fast a - sleep.

Play in Harmony

In the last lesson, you learned to sing a melodic ostinato. This time, you can **play** ostinatos that go with "Tender Shepherd."

Alto Metallophone

Bass Xylophone

M·U·S·I·C M·A·K·E·R·S

Mary Martin

Mary Martin (1913–1990) began her career teaching dance, and singing on the radio, in her home state of Texas. She moved to New York to perform in several Broadway plays, then went to Hollywood to try movie acting. Martin starred in ten films. She returned to theater in 1949 and performed in many shows. Her most famous roles were the leads in *South Pacific* and *Peter Pan*.

Review, Assess,

What Do You Know?

1. You're the composer, and you're making decisions about how you want your string quartet to sound.

   a. If you want the musicians to play so that the notes sound short or separated, tell them to play _____.
      1) *legato*   2) *staccato*

   b. If you want the musicians to play so that the notes sound connected and smooth, tell them to play _____.
      1) *legato*   2) *staccato*

   c. If you want the music to sound *staccato*, ask them to play _____.
      1) *arco*   2) *pizzicato*

   d. For *legato* sounds, ask them to play _____.
      1) *arco*   2) *pizzicato*

2. Read these rhythms. Which ones last for one beat?

   a. ♩   **b.** ♩   **c.** ♬♬   **d.** 𝄽   **e.** ♫

What Do You Hear? 3

 CD 4–24

You will hear three examples of string instruments.
Point to the word that matches the instrument you hear.

    1. string bass   viola
    2. string bass   viola
    3. viola   violin

Perform, Create

What You Can Do

Move with the Music

Listen to the recording of *Gavotte* on page 88. Move to match each section of the piece. Use short movements for the *staccato* sections, and smoother movements for the *legato* section.

Create an Ostinato

Create a simple rhythm ostinato to accompany *"Hwa yuan li-de young wa wa"* on page 102.

- Choose from these rhythms for your four-beat ostinato.

- Perform your ostinato softly using body percussion as you sing.

- Then perform your ostinato on nonpitched percussion instruments. Choose instruments with timbres that match the song.

Improvise a Melody

Improvise a melody for your rhythm ostinato. Use these pitches. Begin and end on F or C.

Rhythm Skill Builder

Here's a way to practice your rhythm skills and get on your feet! Choose a line of this speech piece to learn. Put your part together with classmates to **perform** this famous tongue-twister.

CD 4–27

How Much Wood Could a Woodchuck Chuck

Setting by Grace Nash

Building Our Musical Skills

Singing the Blues

There is a legend about Groundhog Day. If a groundhog sees its shadow on February 2, there will be six more weeks of winter. If not, spring will come early.

Sing "The Groundhog Blues." What happens?

CD 4–29

The Groundhog Blues

Words and Music by Gayle Giese

With a swing

The ground - hog crept right out of the log, ___

The sun shone down, bright on that hog. ___

The ground - hog was a hog of small brain, ___

He did not know his Sha - dow by name. ___

Hog met Sha - dow and said in fright, ___

Moving Fast and Slow

Before pipes were installed to bring water into houses, people got water from wells in the ground. To "draw" a bucket of water meant to pull the bucket up out of the well.

Listen for a tempo change as you **sing** the song.

CD 4–31
MIDI 12

Draw Me a Bucket of Water

African American Singing Game

Moderato

Draw me a buck-et of wa-ter,

For my old-est daugh-ter,

We got none in the bunch, We're all out the bunch,
one   and three
two   and two
three   and one

You go un-der sis-ter Sal-ly.

DRAW ME A BUCKET OF WATER Written and adapted by Bessie Jones. Collected and Edited by Alan Lomax. TRO–© Copyright 1972 (Renewed) Ludlow Music, Inc., New York, N.Y. Used by permission.

Allegro

F ... Bb ... F

Frog in the buck-et and I can't get him out,

F ... Bb ... F

Frog in the buck-et and I can't get him out,

F

Frog in the buck-et and I can't get him out,

Bb ... F ... C ... F ... *Repeat 1 time*

Frog in the buck-et and I can't get him out.

Hurry Up!

You know that tempo is the speed of the beat. In the recording of "Draw Me a Bucket of Water," you hear a **subito** tempo change between the two sections of the song. Does the music get faster or slower?

Subito means "sudden."

Be a Bucket!

This game lets you become the bucket!

◀ *Draw me a bucket of water.*

Two in the bunch, and two out the bunch. ▶

Frog in the bucket and I can't get him out.

Listen to this instrumental piece by William Grant Still, an African American composer. Does the tempo change or stay the same?

CD 4–34
Ennanga, Movement III

by William Grant Still

An *ennanga* is a kind of harp from Uganda, a country in Africa.

Sing with Strong Beats

"Morning Is Come" is a perfect way to wake up your voice. **Listen** to "Morning Is Come." Then **sing** the song.

CD 4–35

Morning Is Come

Round from England

Morn - ing   is   come,   night   is   a - way,

Rise   with   the   sun _____ and __ wel - come   the   day.

How many beats are in each group of birds below?
Tap the beats as you **sing** the song again.

Groups of Three

This song moves in a pattern of three beats, one strong beat and two weak beats.

Create your own motions to show this pattern of strong and weak beats. Be sure the first beat feels strong!

One Sound, Three Beats

You already know this two-beat note. ♩

You also know this one-beat note. ♩

These notes tied together last for three beats. It can be written like this. ♩‿♩

It can also be written like this. ♩.

Find the ♩. in the music. Then **sing** the song while you do a pat-clap-clap pattern.

Beats and Bar Lines

Follow the rhythms below as you **listen** to "The Juniper Tree." Look for the note that gets three beats. What looks different about this music?

Oh, sis - ter Phoe - be, how mer - ry were we, The

night we sat un - der the jun - i - per tree, The

jun - i - per tree, hi - o, hi - o, The

jun - i - per tree, hi - o.

Tune In

Juniper trees can be as short as shrubs and as tall as giant cypress trees.

Add the Bar Lines

Bar lines are drawn to show how beats are grouped together in music. The space between two bar lines is called a **measure.** The number "3" at the beginning of this song shows that there are three beats in each measure. A **double bar line** means you have reached the end of the song.

Sing "The Juniper Tree" and look for the bar lines.

The Juniper Tree

CD 4–40

Folk Song from Arkansas

bar line

measure

double bar line

1. Oh, sis - ter Phoe - be, how mer - ry were we, The
2. Go choose a part - ner, so choose you a one, Go

night we sat un - der the jun - i - per tree, The
choose you the fair - est that ev - er you can. Now

jun - i - per tree, hi - o, hi - o, The
rise you up, gal, and go, and go, Now

jun - i - per tree, hi - o.
rise you up, gal, and go.

Copyright 1937 by John A. Lomax.
Reprinted by permission of Global Jukebox Publishing.

Enjoying Rhythm

Think about the place where you live. What do you like best? **Listen** to *"¡Qué gusto!"* What does the singer like about living in the country?

CD 4–45

¡Qué gusto!
(What Pleasure)

English Words by Ruth De Cesare (adapted)   Hispanic Song of the American Southwest

¡Qué gus - to,   qué gus - to,   qué gus - to   me   da,
What pleas - ure,   what plea - sure   and   joy   it   gives   me

vi - vir   en   el   cam - po   con   tran - qui - li - dad!
To   live   in   the   coun - try,   so   peace - ful   and   free!

Yo   can - to,   yo   brin - co   a   mi   li - ber - tad,
I   sing   and   I   dance   and   I   jump   all   a - round,

por - que   no   hay   ti - je - ras   de   la   so - cie - dad.
Ver - y   free   of   the   crowds and   the   noise   I   once   found.

Move to the Country

Look at the beginning of the song. What do you see before the first bar line? This note is called the **upbeat**. **Sing** the song and **move** to show the upbeat.

An **upbeat** is one or more notes before the first strong beat of a phrase.

Si me pongo yo a cantar

Translated by Joseph F. Domínguez

If I begin to sing
For a whole year long
Not once will I be heard
Repeating the same song.

Si me pongo yo a cantar
Un año y sus doce meses,
No me han de sentir echar
La misma canción dos veces.

Show What You Know!

Practice saying the rhythms below with rhythm syllables. Then **perform** them with two classmates. Which of these rhythms has an upbeat? Be ready to explain your answer.

1.
2.
3.

Around and AROUND and Around

Listen to "*Doong gul ge,*" a Korean singing game. It has two sections, **A** and **B**, but you sing the **A** section twice. This is called **A** **B** **A** form.

CD 4–49

Doong gul ge

('Round and Around We Go)

English Words by Kim Williams

Korean Words and Music by Lee Su In

둥 글 게 둥 글 게 (손뼉) 둥 글 게 둥 글 게 (손뼉)
Doong gul ge doong gul ge, *doong gul ge doong gul ge,*
'Round and a-round we go, 'round and a-round we go!

빙 글 빙 글 돌 아 가 며 춤 을 춥 시 다 (손뼉)
bing gul bing gul dol ah kah miaw chum ul chup shi da.
Dance a-round the cir - cle now, don't let your feet be slow.

손 뼉 을 치 면 서 (손뼉) 노 래 를 부 르 며 (손뼉)
Son bia kul chi mian sawh, *no reh rul pu ru miaw,*
Cir - cle a-round and clap, cir - cle a-round and sing,

랄 랄 랄 라 즐 거 웁 게 춤 추 자
la la la la chul kaw up ge chum chu cha.
Let's all run to - geth - er now a - round the ring!

China

Korean
Peninsula ▶

Tune In

North Korea and South Korea are on a peninsula. A peninsula is land surrounded by water on three sides.

B

G   C   G

링 가 링 가 링   가 링 가 링 가 링

Ring - a - ring - a - ring _____ a - ring - a - ring - a - ring,
Ring - a - ring - a - ring _____ a - ring - a - ring - a - ring,

D

링 가 링 가 링   가 링 가 링 가 링

ring - a - ring - a - ring _____ a - ring - a - ring - a - ring.
ring - a - ring - a - ring _____ a - ring - a - ring - a - ring.

G   D   C

손 에 손 을 잡   고 모 두 다 함 께

Son eh son ul chah(p) _ go mo du da hahm ge,
Hop - ping as we go   and jump - ing as we sing,

D.C. al Fine

G   D

즐 거 웁 게 춤 을 춤 시 다 _____

chul kaw up ge chum ul chup shi da. _____
Let's all run to - geth - er 'round the ring! _____

Move Around

Learn to play a singing game that goes with *"Doong gul ge."*

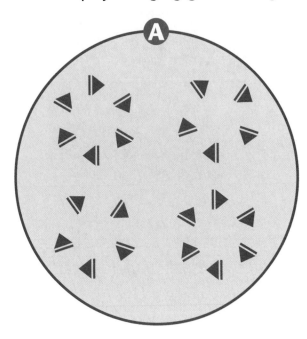

A Walk in small circles. Change direction whenever you hear hand claps in the music. Clap your hands too!

B Join in a big circle. Jump in and out when you hear *"Son eh son ul chop"* or *"Hopping as we go."*

Arts Connection

◄ This porcelain jar with iron-brown underglaze was made in Korea in the 1700s.

Music of Korea

The *kayagum* [kah-YAH-guhm] is a Korean folk instrument. The term *kayagum pyongch'ang* describes a person playing the *kayagum* and singing with his or her instrument.

Listen to this traditional Korean music.

CD 4–53

Kayagum pyongch'ang-sae t'aryug

Traditional Korean

This piece is an example of Korean music that has four thousand years of tradition.

kayagum
▼

Forms of Morning

Roosters crow before the day begins. What sounds wake you up in the morning? **Listen** for the **introduction** and **coda** in "*Kum bachur atzel.*"

An **introduction** is music that is played before the words are sung.

A **coda** is music that ends a song after the words are sung.

CD 5–1
MIDI 13

Kum bachur atzel
(Hear the Rooster Crowing)

English Words by David ben Avraham   *Folk Song from Israel*

Kum   ba - chur   a - tzel ___   v' - tzei   la - a - vo - da,
Hear the roost - er crow - ing,   A - crow - ing at   the dawn;

Kum   ba - chur   a - tzel ___   v' - tzei   la - a - vo - da;
Hear the roost - er crow - ing,   A - crow - ing at   the dawn.

Kum,   kum, ___   v' - tzei   la - a - vo - da.
Wake,   wake, ___   for   now   the night has gone;

Kum,   kum, ___   v' - tzei   la - a - vo - da.
Wake,   wake, ___   for   now   the night has gone.

Play with the Rooster

Create a new introduction and coda for this song. Use instruments that make morning sounds. **Play** your music.

Then **play** this accompaniment for *"Kum bachur atzel."*

Alto Xylophone

Bass Xylophone

More Music from Israel

Now **listen** to *Tzlil Zugim*. Notice the introduction, and **listen** for the coda at the end.

CD 5–5
Tzlil Zugim

Traditional from Israel

This song is often performed for dancing.

Ku - ku - ri - ku, ku - ku - ri - ku, tar - n' - gol ka - ra;
Ku - ku - ri - ku, ku - ku - ri - ku, yawn a might - y yawn;

Ku - ku - ri - ku, ku - ku - ri - ku, tar - n' - gol ka - ra.
Ku - ku - ri - ku, ku - ku - ri - ku, yawn a might - y yawn.

New Pitch in the House

"Li'l Liza Jane" is a verse and refrain
song from the United States. **Listen**
for a new pitch in "Li'l Liza Jane."

CD 5–6
MIDI 14

Li'l Liza Jane

Dance Song from the United States

VERSE

1. I got a house in Bal - ti - more, Li'l Li - za Jane,
2. I got a house in Bal - ti - more, Li'l Li - za Jane,

Street - car runs right by my door, Li'l Li - za Jane.
Brus - sels car - pet on the floor, Li'l Li - za Jane.

Start on a High Note

The refrain of "Li'l Liza Jane" begins with a new pitch. Does it sound higher or lower than the pitches in the verse?

The new pitch is called *high do* (*do*^l), just like the *do* you already know. What is different about this pitch?

do   re   mi   so   la   do^l

Now **sing** the refrain with pitch syllables and hand signs. You already know the hand sign for the new pitch!

REFRAIN

C   G₇

Oh,   E - li - za,   Li'l   Li - za   Jane,

C   G₇   C

Oh,   E - li - za,   Li'l   Li - za   Jane.

3. I got a house in Baltimore,
    Li'l Liza Jane,
    Silver doorplate on the door,
    Li'l Liza Jane.

4. Come, my love, and be with me,
    Li'l Liza Jane,
    And I'll take good care of thee,
    Li'l Liza Jane.

Hop Up to a High Note

This is a song from the days before automobiles! **Listen** to discover how many ladies fit in the buggy. Then **sing** the song.

CD 5–11

Hop Up, My Ladies

Folk Song from the United States

VERSE
D — G — D

do

1. Did you e - ver go to meet-ing, Un - cle Joe, Un - cle Joe?

D — A₇

Did you e - ver go to meet - ing, Un - cle Joe? ___

D — G — D

Did you e - ver go to meet-ing, Un - cle Joe, Un - cle Joe?

G — D A₇ D

I don't mind the weath-er, if the wind don't blow.

Collected, adapted and arranged by John A. Lomax and Alan Lomax. TRO © Copyright 1941 (Renewed) Ludlow Music;, Inc., New York, N. Y. Used by permission.

From *do* to High *do*

Sing these pitches with hand signs and pitch syllables. Point to *high do*.

do   re   mi   so   la   do'

Now **sing** the refrain of the song with pitch syllables. Notice the leap from *do* to *high do*. The distance from *do* to *high do* is called an **octave.**

An **octave** is the distance between one note and the next higher or lower note that has the same name.

REFRAIN

Hop up, my la - dies, three in a row,

Hop up, my la - dies, three in a row,

Hop up, my la - dies, three in a row,

I don't mind the weath - er if the wind don't blow.

2. Will your horse carry double,
   Uncle Joe, Uncle Joe? . . .
   Refrain

3. Is your horse a single footer,
   Uncle Joe, Uncle Joe? . . .
   Refrain

Music from the Movies

Listen to the very beginning of this piece to hear the first octave leap. It goes by quickly! Then **listen** for *high do* in the theme shown below.

CD 5–16
The Magnificent Seven

by Elmer Bernstein

The Magnificent Seven is an American western movie from 1960. This piece from the movie score is one of Bernstein's best-known works.

The Magnificent Seven
Listening Map

The *Magnificent Seven* was one of many western movies released in the United States in the 1960s and 1970s. Each movie had its own unique musical score.

M·U·S·I·C M·A·K·E·R·S

Elmer Bernstein

Elmer Bernstein (born 1922) has written the music for many movies over the last 40 years. He graduated from The Juilliard School of Music in New York. His first major movie score was the Frank Sinatra movie, *The Man with the Golden Arm*. He also wrote the music for *Ghostbusters* and *To Kill a Mockingbird*. His music mixes American classical style with jazz.

Take It to the Net Go to *www.sfsuccessnet.com* to learn more about music for the movies.

Sing and Play Together

"Walk Together, Children" is a spiritual in which you sing *high do*. **Listen** to the song. The first note of the song is *so*. The last note of the song is *do*. Where is *high do*?

CD 5–17
MIDI 15

Walk Together, Children

African American Spiritual

Swing style

1. Oh, walk to-geth-er, chil-dren, Don't you get __ wea - ry,
2. Oh, talk to-geth-er, chil-dren, Don't you get __ wea - ry,

Walk to-geth-er, chil-dren, Don't you get wea - ry,
Talk to-geth-er, chil-dren, Don't you get wea - ry,

Oh, walk to-geth-er, chil-dren, Don't you get __ wea - ry,
Oh, talk to-geth-er, chil-dren, Don't you get __ wea - ry,

There's a great camp-meet-ing in the prom-ised land. __
There's a great camp-meet-ing in the prom-ised land. __

3. Oh, sing together, children, . . .   4. Oh, shout together, children, . . .

146

Create and Play

Create percussion ostinatos to accompany this song. Make up a different ostinato for each verse.

Now add this melodic ostinato that includes both *do* and *high do.* **Play** it on a keyboard or bells.

(Repeat 6 times)

Show What You Know!

1. Here are all of the pitches you know. **Sing** from *do* to *high do* and back again.

do   re   mi   so   la   do[|]

2. Where is *high do?* For each *do,* point to the place on the staff where you would expect to find *high do.* Use the first example as a guide.

do   high do   do   high do?   do   high do?

3. Look back! Find the *high do* in either "Li'l Liza Jane," on page 140 or "Hop Up, My Ladies," on page 142. **Sing** the phrases that include *high do* using pitch syllables.

Mallet Magic

Some percussion instruments have bars arranged like a piano keyboard. The bars are played with mallets. Mallets are sticks with rubber, felt, wood, or yarn balls on one end.

Meet the Xylophone

The xylophone is one of the oldest mallet instruments. *Xylophone* means "wood sound." The bars of a xylophone are made out of wood.

▼ xylophone (orchestral)

Xylophone Sound

Listen to this xylophone solo played by Evelyn Glennie.

CD 5–19
Whirlwind

by Joe Green

A brass band plays the accompaniment in this recording.

CD 5–20
Interview with Evelyn Glennie

MUSIC MAKERS
Evelyn Glennie

Evelyn Glennie (born 1965) was born in Aberdeen, Scotland. When she was twelve years old, she began playing percussion instruments. Now she performs with musicians in many countries and from many cultures. Glennie is one of only a few female solo percussionists in the world.

Video Library See an eight-year-old play mallet instruments in *Percussion Instruments: Tuned.*

Marimba Magic

The marimba is similar to the xylophone, but it has long resonating tubes that hang below each bar. The marimba has a more mellow sound than the xylophone.

Listen to *Memories of the Seashore*, played by Keiko Abe [KAY-ko AH-bay]. How would you **describe** a marimba's sound?

▼ marimba (orchestral)

CD 5–21

Memories of the Seashore

written and performed by Keiko Abe

Abe imagined the ocean as she wrote this piece.

M·U·S·I·C M·A·K·E·R·S

Keiko Abe

Keiko Abe (born 1937) is a Japanese marimba virtuoso, composer, teacher, and music arranger for percussion. She was born in Tokyo and played piano and xylophone as a child. She began composing at a young age. She chose the marimba as her main instrument when she was twelve years old. Abe also designs marimbas. She was one of Evelyn Glennie's teachers.

Lionel Hampton

Lionel Hampton (1913–2002) was born in Louisville, Kentucky. When he was a boy he joined a drum and bugle corps. As he got older, he played in jazz groups and learned to play the marimba. Jazz trumpeter Louis Armstrong encouraged Hampton to try the vibraphone, or "vibes." Soon Hampton formed his own band, featuring the vibes. Lionel Hampton's band was one of the most famous of the swing era.

More Magic

The vibraphone has metal bars and a resonating tube below each bar. A small, electric motor in the tube spins a metal fan when a switch is turned on. The spinning fan makes the vibrating sound.

Listen to Lionel Hampton play the vibraphone in the jazz composition *Pick-a-Rib*.

CD 5–22
Pick-a-Rib

by Goodman and Hampton

The vibraphone has been used in many kinds of ensembles. It was a very popular instrument in the early days of jazz.

Partner Songs

Here is a song you may already know. **Sing** "This Old Man." Get ready for a special challenge!

CD 5–23

This Old Man

Folk Song from England

1. This old man, he played one, He played nick-nack on my drum.
2. This old man, he played two, He played nick-nack on my shoe.

Nick-nack pad-dy-whack, give the dog a bone. This old man came roll-ing home.

3. . . . three, He played nick-nack on my tree.

4. . . . four, He played nick-nack on my door.

5. . . . five, He played nick-nack on my hive.

6. . . . six, He played nick-nack on my sticks.

7. . . . seven, He played nick-nack on my oven.

8. . . . eight, He played nick-nack on my gate.

9. . . . nine, He played nick-nack on my line.

10. . . . ten, He played nick-nack on my hen.

Begin a New Song

Now learn a new song. **Listen** for the nonsense words in "Michael Finnigan," then **sing** along.

CD 5–25

Michael Finnigan

Traditional from the United States

1. There was an old man named Mi - chael Fin - ni - gan,
2. There was an old man named Mi - chael Fin - ni - gan,
3. There was an old man named Mi - chael Fin - ni - gan,

He had whis - kers on his chin - ni - gan, The
He went fish - ing with a pin - ni - gan, He
Climbed a tree and barked his shin - ni - gan, He

wind came up and blew them in a - gain,
caught a fish but dropped it in a - gain,
lost a - bout a yard of skin - ni - gan,

Poor old Mi - chael Fin - ni - gan. Be - gin a - gain.

4. There was an old man named Michael Finnigan,
He grew fat and then grew thinnigan,
Then he died and had to begin again,
Poor old Michael Finnigan. Begin again.

A Special Challenge!

Sing "This Old Man" and "Michael Finnigan" as partner songs. **Sing** one song with half of your class while the rest of the class sings the other song.

One Song, Two Melodies

Plants need sun and rain to grow. What do you need to grow?

Sing "Each of Us Is a Flower."

CD 5–28

Each of Us Is a Flower

Words and Music by Charlotte Diamond

Each of us ____ is a flow - er,

Grow-ing in ____ life's ____ gar - den. ____

Each of us ____ is a flow - er,

We need ____ the sun ____ and rain.

Making Beautiful Music

"Each of Us Is a Flower" can be sung as a partner song with itself. Sing the first melody **A**. Then practice the second melody **B**. Then sing the two melodies at the same time to form a partner song.

B

F   B♭   C₇   F
Sun, _____ shine your warmth on __ me.

F   B♭   C₇   F
Moon, _____ cool me with your _ night.

F   B♭   C₇   F
Wind, _____ bring the gen - tle __ rain.

F   B♭   C₇   F
Earth, _____ dig my roots down deep.

Review, Assess,

What Do You Know?

1. Look at the notation for "Hop Up, My Ladies" on page 142.

   a. Point to two places in the song where each of the following pitches occurs.

   so   la   mi   re   high do

   b. Point to a bar line in the music.

   c. Point to the double bar line.

2. *Subito* means

   a. fast   **b.** sudden   **c.** gradual

3. Look at the photographs below.

   a. Point to the instruments with bars made of wood.

   b. Point to the instrument with bars made of metal.

What Do You Hear? 4

CD 5–30

You will hear three different mallet instruments. Point to the word that matches the instrument you hear.

1. xylophone   marimba   vibraphone

2. xylophone   marimba   vibraphone

3. xylophone   marimba   vibraphone

▲ vibraphone

▲ xylophone   ▲ marimba

Perform, Create

What You Can Do

Sing a Partner Song

Sing "Each of Us Is a Flower" on page 154.

- First, everyone sings the **A** section followed by the **B** section.

- Then sing both sections at the same time, with a different group singing each section.

- Always sing with good vocal quality.

- Make sure that both melodies are heard when they are sung together.

Create Music

Create an introduction and a coda for "Each of Us Is a Flower."

- Choose a rhythm pattern from the song to use in your introduction and coda.

- What instruments will you use to match the style of the song?

Scat, Scat, What's All That?

One style of jazz singing is called scat. Scat is a style of jazz singing where nonsense syllables take the place of words.

Listen to the melody of *The Flat Foot Floogee* and **sing** the scat words. Then **move** your shoes on the floor to play a scat game.

CD 5–33

The Flat Foot Floogee

by Slim Gaillard, Slam Stewart, and Bud Green

A recording of this song was placed in a time capsule at the 1939 World's Fair. It will be opened in the year 5000.

Discovering new Musical Horizons

Singing with Style

Sing "The Flat Floogee." Then **sing** the song again and **create** your own scat syllables.

The Flat Foot Floogee

Words and Music by Slim Gaillard,
Slam Stewart, and Bud Green

The flat foot floo - gee with the floy floy, ___
The flat foot floo - gee with the flou* flou, ___

The flat foot floo - gee with the floy floy, ___
The flat foot floo - gee with the flou flou, ___

The flat foot floo - gee with the floy floy, ___
The flat foot floo - gee with the flou flou, ___

Floy doy, __ floy doy, __ floy doy, __ floy doy. __
Flou dow, _ flou dow, _ flou dow, _ flou dow. _

*Rhymes with "how"

160

If you're feel - in' low-down, Don't know what to do, __

D.C. al Fine

And you want a show-down, Here's the on - ly dance for you. __

MUSIC MAKERS
"Slim" Gaillard and "Slam" Stewart

Bulee "Slim" Gaillard (1916–1991) and **Leroy "Slam" Stewart** (1914–1987) were known for their own style of high-energy jazz. They first met in New York City in 1936. "Slam" had already developed his own fun jazz style. The team was known as "Slim and Slam." They were popular on the top radio shows of the day.

Dynamic Choices

How do you decide how loudly or how softly to sing a song? Look for clues in the words of this song that tell you what dynamics you might choose.

CD 5–36
MIDI 16

Hush, Hush

African American Spiritual

1. Hush,   hush,   some-bod-y's call-in' my name,
2. Who,   who,   who, Lord, is call-in' my name?

Hush,   hush,   some-bod-y's call-in' my   name, _____
Who,   who,   who, Lord, is call-in' my   name? _____

Hush,   hush,   some-bod-y's call-in' my name,
Who,   who,   who, Lord, is call-in' my name?

Oh, my Lord, _ oh, my Lord, _ what shall I do? ___
Oh, my Lord, _ oh, my Lord, _ what shall I do? ___

3. You, you, you, Lord, are callin' my name, . . .

Singing Sounds

 to this piece. How would you describe the dynamics in this song?

CD 5–38
Alleluia

**from *Mass for the 21st Century*
by Carman Moore**

This work was recorded live in New York City.

Meet the Composer

Listen to Carman Moore discuss his work.

CD 5–39
Interview with Carman Moore

M·U·S·I·C M·A·K·E·R·S

Carman Moore

Carman Moore (born 1936) is from Ohio. He studied French horn, cello, and music history at The Ohio State University. Later he moved to New York City, where he studied composition at The Juilliard School of Music. His compositions include works for orchestra, opera, theater, dance, and film.

The *Mass for the 21st Century* was written for and performed at Lincoln Center in New York City. It has also been performed in South Africa, Australia, and Japan.

MIDI Change the dynamics in the MIDI song file for "Hush, Hush."

Show Some Spirit!

"Do, Lord" has two sections, a verse and a refrain. Which section is repeated? How are the dynamics in this song different from "Hush, Hush"?

Play this accompaniment on the refrain of "Do, Lord."

Do, Lord

African American Spiritual

Do, Lord, oh do, Lord, oh do re-mem-ber me,

Do, Lord, oh do, Lord, oh do re-mem-ber me.

Do, Lord, oh do, Lord, oh do re-mem-ber me,

Rit. last time

Look a-way be-yond ___ the blue.

164

Add a Part

Play this accompaniment on the verse of the song.

I got a home in glo-ry land that out-shines the sun,

I got a home in glo-ry land that out-shines the sun.

I got a home in glo-ry land that out-shines the sun,

Look a-way be-yond ___ the blue.

Working Rhythms

Before machines were invented to do heavy labor, these jobs were done by large groups of workers. Why would they not want the captain's watch to run down and stop?

Listen for different rhythms as you **sing** the song.

Don't Let Your Watch Run Down

CD 6–3

Work Song from South Texas

REFRAIN

Don't let your watch run down, Cap - tain,

Don't let your watch run down. _____

1. Wor - kin' on the lev - ee, dol - lar and a half a day,

Wor - kin' on the lev - ee, draw - in' my pay.

2. Workin' on the railroad, mud up to my knees,
   Workin' on the railroad, tryin' to please. *Refrain*

3. When you see me comin', hoist your window high,
   When you see me leavin', bow down and cry. *Refrain*

Rhythms to Read

This song has rhythm patterns you know. Find each rhythm that lasts for one beat. Then find each pattern that lasts for two beats. Where is the pattern that lasts for three beats? HINT: Look for a tie.

Show What You Know!

Say the rhythms below, using rhythm syllables. How many beats are in each train car?

Frontier Rhythms

In the frontier days of America, people danced for entertainment. Going to a dance was a way to meet neighbors and relax. Here's a frontier song you can still dance to today. **Listen** to "Coffee Grows on White Oak Trees."

CD 6–8

Coffee Grows on White Oak Trees

Folk Song from the United States

REFRAIN

Cof - fee grows on white oak trees.

The riv - er flows with hon - ey - o.

Go choose some - one to roam with you,

As sweet as m'las - ses can - dy - o.

Two or Three?

Which section of this song is written in meter in 3? Which section is in meter in 2?

Partners in Rhythm

Pick a partner and choose two different instruments. As you **sing** this song, **play** on the first beat of each measure. Your partner then plays the other beat or beats in the measure on his or her instrument.

VERSE

1. Two in the mid - dle and they can't go o - ver,

Two in the mid - dle and they can't go o - ver,

Two in the mid - dle and they can't go o - ver,

Hel - lo, Su - san Brown.

2. Swing you another one and you'll get over,   *(3 times)*
   Hello, Susan Brown.   *Refrain*

3. Four in the middle and they all go over,   *(3 times)*
   Hello, Susan Brown.   *Refrain*

Waltzing Bear Rhythms

This comical song is about someone who likes to waltz with bears. What is the meter of the song? Follow the paw prints on the edge of the page with your finger as you **listen** to the recording. Why are some of the paw prints bigger than others?

CD 6–14

Waltzing with Bears

Words and Music by Dale Marxen

REFRAIN

He goes wa - wa - wa - wa - wa, waltz - ing with bears,

Rag - gy bears, bag - gy bears, shag - gy bears, too.

There's noth - ing on earth Un - cle Wal - ter won't do

So he can go waltz - ing, wa - wa - wa - waltz - ing,

So he can go waltz - ing, waltz - ing with bears.

Fine

1. I went to his room in the mid-dle of the night,
I tip-toed in-side and turned on the light,
But to my dis-may, he was no-where in sight,
My un-cle Wal-ter goes waltz-ing at night.

Coda (Freely)

Now he's waltz-ing with pan-das, and we don't un-der-stand it,
But the bears all de-mand at least one waltz a day!

2. We bought Uncle Walter a new coat to wear,
   But when he comes home it's all covered with hair,
   And lately I've noticed there are several new tears,
   My uncle Walter goes waltzing with bears.   *Refrain*

3. We told Uncle Walter that he should be good,
   And do all the things we say that he should,
   But I know that he'd rather be off in the woods,
   We're afraid we will lose him, we'll lose him for good.   *Refrain*

4. We said, "Uncle Walter, oh, please won't you stay,"
   And managed to keep him at home for a day,
   But the bears all barged in and they took him away.   *(to Coda)*

Listen to a Bear Dance

Listen to this piece by Béla Bartók and tap the beats on the listening map. What is the meter of this piece?

CD 6–16
Bear Dance

from _Ten Easy Pieces_
by Béla Bartók

Bartók wrote this piece to help students learn to play the piano.

Bear Dance
Listening Map

(continues)

ending (1:36)

M·U·S·I·C M·A·K·E·R·S

Béla Bartók

Béla Bartók (1881–1945) is Hungary's most famous composer. He studied piano and composition at the Royal Academy in Budapest. In the early 1900s he traveled around Hungary listening to folk songs. He included many of these melodies and rhythms in his compositions. The *Ten Easy Pieces* are all based on folk melodies and folk rhythms.

Waltz Like a Bear

Imagine that you are a bear in "Waltzing with Bears." Stand on your hind legs and take a heavy step with your right foot. Then lightly step left-right. Repeat, beginning with your left foot. Hold up your front paws and sway!

A NEW FORM

Listen to discover the form of this song.

CD 6–17
MIDI 18

Railroad Corral

Cowboy Song from the United States

(A)

1. We're up in the morn - ing 'ere break - ing of day,
2. Come take up your cin - ches, come shake out your reins,

The chuck wag - on's bus - y, the flap - jacks in play;
Come wake your old bron - co and break for the plains.

(A)

The herds are a - stir ov - er hill - side and dale
Come rout out your steer from the long chap - ar - ral,

The night rid - ers push - ing them on to the trail.
The out - fit is off to the rail - road cor - ral.

Cowhand Talk

railroad corral — a railroad station from which cattle are shipped to market

chuck wagon — a portable kitchen on a cart

cinch — a strap used to hold a saddle on a horse

rawhide — a whip made of untanned cowhide

chaparral — a thicket of shrubs and thorny bushes

bronco — a wild horse found in the western United States

In the 1800s cowhands were usually men, but today both men and women work as cowhands.

B
G   C

Whoo-pi - ti - yi - ay,   whoo-pi - ti - yi - ay!
Whoo-pi - ti - yi - ay,   whoo-pi - ti - yi - ay!

D   G

Swing out your raw - hides and give them full play.
Swing out your raw - hides and give them full play.

A
G   C

We're up in the morn - ing 'ere break - ing of day,
Come take up your cin - ches, come shake out your reins,

D   G

The chuck wag - on's bus - y, the flap - jacks in play.
Come wake your old bron - co and break for the plains.

Move Along the Trail

Move to show the form of "Railroad Corral."

First and last Ⓐ sections:
Walk in time with the music, taking two steps per measure.

Second Ⓐ section:
Walk in a different direction.

Ⓑ section:
Stand in place and swing your arms.

Arts Connection

The Rattlesnake
by Frederic Remington
(1861–1909)

Remington's paintings and
sculptures show action and
motion. What action do you
see in this sculpture? ▶

Sounds of the West

Listen to discover the form of this well-known American
music. **Create** movement to show the form.

CD 6–19
Cattle

from *The Plow That Broke the Plains*
by Virgil Thomson

This piece combines three cowboy waltz melodies.

Soaring Melodies

"Now Let Me Fly" is an African American spiritual. Many spirituals speak of flying away. During the time of slavery, to "fly away" often meant to escape to freedom.

Listen to the recording. **Sing** pitch syllables with the refrain. How many different pitches are there?

CD 6–20
MIDI 19

Now Let Me Fly

African American Spiritual

REFRAIN

Now let me fly, _____ Now let me fly, _____

Now let me fly _____ way up high, _

Way in the mid-dle of the air.

Pentatonic Passage

Here are all of the pitches in "Now Let Me Fly."

so₁   la₁   do   re   mi   so   la

Since there are only five different pitches, this is a pentatonic song. What other pentatonic songs do you know?

VERSE

1. Way down yon - der in the mid - dle of the field,

See me work - in' at the char - iot wheel.

Not so par - tic - 'lar 'bout work - in' at the wheel,

D.C. al Fine

But I just wan - na see how the char - iot feels.

2. I got a mother in the Promised Land,
   Ain't gonna stop 'til I shake her hand.
   Not so partic'lar 'bout shakin' her hand,
   But I just wanna get up to the Promised Land.

The Wind Blows Home

"Don't Let the Wind" is an African American folk song from an island off the Atlantic coast of the United States. The song starts on *mi*. **Listen** to the song. On what pitch does the song end?

CD 6–22

Don't Let the Wind

Folk Song from St. Helena Island

Don't let the wind, don't let the wind, don't let the wind blow here no more.

Oh, _____ don't let the wind, don't let the wind blow here no more.

Sailing on a Melody

All of these pitches are in "Don't Let the Wind." Since the song ends on *do*, we say that *do* is the home tone. Read these notes.

do   re   mi   so   la   do'

Find these pitches in the song. Then **sing** the song with pitch syllables and hand signs.

Show What You Know!

Each of the melodies below is from a song you know. What is the home tone in each?

1.

2.

3.

Tune In

St. Helena Island is off the coast of South Carolina. It is part of the United States.

A New Home Tone

"Erdö, erdö de magos" starts on *do*. **Listen** for notes in this song that are lower than *do*.

CD 6–27

Erdö, erdö de magos

(In the Silent Forest)

English Words by Jean Sinor   *Folk Song from Hungary*

1. Erd - ö, erd - ö de ma - gos a te - te - je.
1. In the si - lent for - est sings the lone - ly bird,

Jaj, de ré - gen le - hul - lot a le - ve - le.
Cold winds blow - ing whis - per se - crets nev - er heard,

Jaj, de ré - gen le - hul - lot a le - ve - le.
High a - bove the moon re - flects an i - cy light,

Ár - va ma - dár pár - jat ke - re si ben - ne.
Sha - dows flee - ing swift - ly through the au - tumn night.

2. Buza kozé szállt a dalos pacsirta,
   Mert odafenn a szemeit kisírta.
   Búzavirág, búzakalász árnyában
   Rágondolt a régi, els ö párjára.

2. Through the misty treetop flies the orphaned lark.
   Forest branches creaking stiffly, bare and stark.
   Sadly sounds the plaintive calling high above,
   Calling in the autumn shadows for his love.

Coming Home to *la*

This song has all of the pitches shown below. **Sing** them with pitch syllables.

la,   *do*   *re*   *mi*   *so*   *la*

Now **sing** the song with pitch syllables as you point to each pitch.

Since *la* is the last pitch of the song, we say that *la* is the home tone.

The Night Will Never Stay

by Eleanor Farjeon

The night will never stay,
The night will still go by,
Though with a million stars
You pin it to the sky,
Though you bind it with the blowing wind
And buckle it with the moon,
The night will slip away
Like sorrow or a tune.

Flutes of the World

The flute is one of the oldest known instruments. Some type of flute is played in almost every country in the world. Sound is produced in different ways, depending on the type of flute.

Listen to these different flutes.

CD 6–34
Flute Montage

▲ The Western **flute** is usually made of metal.

▲ **Panpipes** are single-tone flutes of different lengths bound together.

▲ The **shakuhachi** [SHAH-koo-HAH-chee] is a bamboo flute from Japan.

▲ The **sao** [dsow] is a bamboo flute from Vietnam.

Beauty in the Wind

Listen to this piece played by Jean-Pierre Rampal, who was one of the finest flutists in the world.

CD 6–35
Sarabande

from *Partita in A Minor*
by Johann Sebastian Bach

Bach wrote music for flute and other solo instruments. He also wrote music for small ensembles and voices.

M·U·S·I·C M·A·K·E·R·S

Jean-Pierre Rampal

Jean-Pierre Rampal (1922–2000) was born in Marseilles, France. His father was a flutist and gave him flute lessons. During World War II, he was in his third year of medical school when the Nazis drafted him. He escaped to Paris instead and attended the National Conservatory. After the war, he became the principal flutist in the Paris Opera Orchestra. Rampal won many awards and played with the world's major symphony orchestras. His wonderful musicianship will be remembered through the recordings he made.

Bring on the Brass!

If you've ever seen a marching band, then you've seen and heard brass instruments. All brass instruments have a mouthpiece, tubing that carries the air, and a bell that makes the sound louder.

Sound is produced when the player "buzzes," or vibrates the lips together while blowing.

Pressing the keys on some brass instruments opens and closes valves. This changes the pitch because the air travels through more or less tubing.

◀ Trombone

▲ Tuba

▲ Trumpet

Build Your Own Brass

To get an idea of how brass instruments work, you can make a simple one using a funnel, a garden hose, and a mouthpiece.

• Insert the funnel into one end of the hose.

• Put the mouthpiece into the other end.

• Roll up the hose to make it easier to handle.

• Buzz your lips into the mouthpiece to make sound.

Tune In

The tubing on brass instruments is all rolled up because otherwise they would be too large to hold. One type of tuba would be eighteen feet long if it were unrolled!

Video Library Watch *Arpeggio Meets the Brass Family* to learn more about them.

Tuba Talk

Listen to Deanna Swoboda discuss her career and her favorite instrument.

CD 6–36

Interview with Deanna Swoboda

M·U·S·I·C M·A·K·E·R·S

Deanna Swoboda

Deanna Swoboda (born 1969) started taking clarinet lessons when she was in the fourth grade. In seventh grade, she decided to learn to play the trombone and then the trumpet. Swoboda added tuba when she was in the eighth grade. Her father helped her carry the instrument to school and to rehearsals. She always wanted to be a professional brass player and teacher, and today she is.

Tuba Tune

Listen to this famous piece. It is usually not played on tuba.

CD 6–37
Flight of the Bumblebee

**by Nikolai Andreyevich Rimsky-Korsakov
as performed by Deanna Swoboda**

This piece for solo instrument is originally from an opera.

The Brass Family

A brass quintet usually consists of 2 trumpets, French horn, trombone, and tuba. **Listen** to a part of Handel's *Water Music* played by Canadian Brass. What words would you use to describe the sound of these instruments?

CD 6–39
Allegro Maestoso

**from *Water Music*
by George Frideric Handel**

Canadian Brass is one of the most famous brass quintets in the world. Each player is also a soloist on his instrument.

▲ Canadian Brass

FUN WITH CANONS

Listen to learn the words of these silly rhymes. Then learn to perform them in **canon.**

Canon is a follow-the-leader process in which all perform the same pattern, but start at different times.

CD 6–41

Table Manners

Anonymous   *Rhythmic Setting by Konnie Saliba*

I raised a great hul - la - ba - loo

when I found a large mouse in my stew.

Said the wait - er, "Don't shout and wave it a - bout,

or the rest will be want - ing one, too!"

There Was an Old Man

Edward Lear

Rhythmic Setting by Konnie Saliba

I
mp

There was an old man with a beard,

II

crescendo to end

who said, "It's just as I feared!

Two owls and a hen, four larks and a wren,

ff

have all built their nests in my beard!"

Speech Texture

Create a piece with many different layers of sound.

• Pat and clap this accompaniment as you speak this piece.

clap
pat

• Now play the accompaniment on low and high timpani.

• Speak the poem once all together, then in a two-part canon.

Play a Morning Song

Here's a song you could use in your classroom every day.
Listen to "Good Morning," and then **sing** it with your class.

CD 7–1
MIDI 20

Good Morning

Words and Music by Elizabeth Gilpatrick

Good morn - ing, good morn - ing, I'm glad you're here to - day.

We'll do our work and have some fun and then go on our way.

You can also **sing** this song in canon. When you sing in canon,
be sure to listen to your part so you don't get lost!

Play and Sing

Play this recorder part while your class **sings** the song.

Canon Call

You can perform "Good Morning" in many different ways.
Try it with and without accompaniment. **Sing** it in unison and
in canon. Which way has the thinnest texture? The thickest?

Singing Together

When singing in parts, you should always

• **Sing** your own part until you know it by heart.

• Practice listening to the second part while you **sing** your own.

• **Listen** to be sure your group is singing in tune.

Listening Together

Listen to *Canon a 4*. Raise your hand as you hear each part enter.

CD 7–3
Canon a 4

from *Musical Offering*
by Johann Sebastian Bach

This recording features two harpsicords.

Review, Assess,

What Do You Know?

1. Name these pitches using pitch syllables.

do

2. Which of these patterns shows AABA form?

   a. ● ■ ▲ ▲   **b.** ● ■ ● ●   **c.** ● ● ■ ●

What Do You Hear? 5A

 CD 7–4

Review the Sound Bank recordings of the instruments listed below. You will then hear three examples of different wind instruments. Point to the name of the instrument you hear.

1. a. flute   **b.** panpipes

2. a. *shakuhachi*   **b.** flute

3. a. trumpet   **b.** tuba

What Do You Hear? 5B

 CD 7–8

You will hear two musical examples. Pat a steady beat to discover the meter of each example.

1. a. $\frac{2}{4}$ **b.** $\frac{3}{4}$

2. a. $\frac{2}{4}$ **b.** $\frac{3}{4}$

Perform, Create

What You Can Do

Create a Canon

Create a speech canon. Work with a partner to write a four-line poem.

- Give lines 1 and 3 the same number of syllables.

- Give lines 2 and 4 the same number of syllables and make them rhyme.

- Decide where the second part of the canon should begin.

- Perform your speech canon for the class. Each of you can perform one part of the canon.

Music Is for Everybody!

Music comes from people all over the world. Many believe music can bring us together to make the world a better place. How can you make the world a better place?

A Peace Corps volunteer teaching students in Botswana. ▶

▲ Teenage volunteers building a house with Habitat for Humanity.

Making Music our own

A National Park Service volunteer inspecting a bird on Alcatraz Island.

Mother Teresa cradling a young orphan. ▶

Everybody Sing!

"I'd Like to Teach the World to Sing" is a song about working to make the world a better place to live. **Listen** to the song. What does the songwriter suggest will make the world better? **Sing** "I'd Like to Teach the World to Sing."

CD 7–9

I'd Like to Teach the World to Sing

Words and Music by Bill Backer, Billy Davis,
Roger Cook, and Roger Greenaway

Swing Style

1. I'd like to teach the world to sing ___ in
2. I'd like to build the world a home ___ and

per - fect har - mo - ny. ___ I'd like to hold it
fur - nish it with love. ___ Grow ap - ple trees and

1., 2. *Fine*

in my arms ___ and keep it com - pa - ny. ___
hon - ey bees ___ and snow-white tur - tle doves. ___

3.

___ That's the song I hear, ___ (That's the song I hear,) ___

Echo the same move. ►

Create Harmony

Find two phrases that echo in "I'd Like to Teach the World to Sing." When different groups of singers perform the echos, they create harmony. **Sing** the song with the echo phrases. Then **create** a movement a friend can echo.

Let the world sing to - day. (Let the world sing to-

day.) A song of peace that

D.C. al Fine—first verse only

e - choes on ___ and nev - er goes a - way. ___

3. I'd like to see the world for once
   All standing hand in hand,
   And hear them echo through the hills
   For peace throughout the land.

Moving from Soft to

If music were always at one dynamic level, it might sound dull.

Composers include symbols in music that tell musicians when to make changes in the dynamic level.

A **crescendo** sign looks like this:

A **decrescendo** sign looks like this:

> A **crescendo** sign tells you to sing or play louder.

> A **decrescendo** sign tells you to sing or play softer.

Volume Control

Symphony conductors have many important jobs. They direct the players when to start and stop. They also help the players remember when to get loud and soft.

MUSIC MAKERS
JoAnn Falletta

JoAnn Falletta (born 1954) is an award-winning conductor. She received a doctorate from The Juilliard School in 1989. She has directed some of the great orchestras of the world, often being the first woman to do so. Falletta is known for conducting new American music. She has been the music director for the Buffalo Philharmonic, the Virginia Symphony, and the Long Beach Symphony orchestras.

Falletta is also known for her classical guitar playing, and has played with many great orchestras.

Loud

Singing-Time

by Rose Fyleman

Dynamics in Action

Follow the dynamic markings as you speak this poem.

I wake in the morning early

And always, the very first thing,

I poke out my head and I sit up in bed

And I sing and I sing and I sing.

Sound Waves

Listen to this piano piece, and raise your hand when you hear a *crescendo*. Where is the piece the loudest? Where is it the softest?

CD 7–11

Valse Noble

**from *Carnaval*
by Robert Schumann**

This composition is one of many Schumann wrote for the piano.

Get on the Level

Find a space to sit on the floor. **Listen** to *Valse Noble.* Show the loudest part of the piece by spreading your arms as far apart as you can. Show the softest part by becoming as small as you can.

Listen one more time. Hold hands with a partner and show the dynamics by growing or shrinking in your space.

Robert Schumann

Robert Schumann (1810–1856) was twenty before he became a serious pianist and composer. He married his piano teacher's daughter, Clara, also a pianist. He wrote many types of music, including piano solos, pieces for ensembles, and songs. Some of his songs and piano pieces were written in sets. *Carnaval* is a set of 21 different piano pieces.

One of his piano sets, *Kinderszenen*, was written especially for children.

Tune In

Clara Schumann was a better-known pianist than her husband. Festivals are still held in Germany to honor her.

Take It to the Net Go to *www.sfsuccessnet.com* to learn more about Robert and Clara Schumann.

Four Beats Together

"Turn the Glasses Over" is a song with meter in 4. This means that there are four beats in each measure, a strong beat followed by three weaker beats.

Create a four-beat movement with one strong beat and three weaker beats. **Sing** the song while you **move**.

 CD 7–12

Turn the Glasses Over

Folk Song from the United States

I've been to Haar - lem, I've been to Do - ver,

I've trav - eled this wide world all o - ver,

O - ver, o - ver, three times o - ver,

Drink what you have to drink and turn the glass - es o - ver.

A Game with Glasses

Play a game with cups or glasses to show meter in 4.
Follow these directions.

1. Pat the bottom of the cup.
2. Pick up your cup.
3. Turn it and tap it on the floor.
4. Pass it to the left.

Sail - ing east, sail - ing west,

Sail - ing o - ver the o - cean,

Bet - ter watch out when the boat be - gins to rock,

Or you'll lose your girl in the o - cean.

UPBEAT OR DOWNBEAT?

In Israel, children plant trees on the holiday called *Tu b'Shvat*. This holiday is like a birthday party for trees.

Tap a steady beat as you **listen** to *"Hashkediya."*

CD 7–17

Hashkediya
(*Tu b'Shvat* Is Here)

Words by M. Dushman   Music by M. Ravina

Hash - ke - di - ya po - ra - hat, V' she-mesh paz zo - ra - hat
The al-mond tree is grow - ing, A gold-en sun is glow - ing;

Tzi - po - rim me - rosh kol gag   M' - vas - rot er bo he - hag;
Birds sing out in joy - ous glee From ev - ery roof and ev - ery tree.

Tu b' Shvat hi - gi - a   Hag ha - i - la - not,
Tu b' Shvat is here, The fes - ti - val of trees.

Tu b' Shvat hi - gi - a   Hag ha - i - la - not.
Hail the trees' New Year. ___ Hap - py ho - li - day!

Pick Up the Beat

In what meter is *"Hashkediya"*? HINT: Look for the number of beats in a measure. Does the song start on an upbeat or **downbeat**?

Tap the beats in each measure as you **sing** the song.

> The **downbeat** is the beat that begins a measure.

Show What You Know!

Create a body percussion ostinato to perform with each rhythm below. Show upbeats and downbeats. How many beats are in each measure?

1. $\frac{2}{4}$

2. $\frac{3}{4}$

3. $\frac{4}{4}$

Tune In

Tu b'Shvat is a holiday for Israeli people to celebrate nature. They plant trees and eat seven foods grown in Israel: wheat, barley, figs, grapes, olives, dates, and pomegranates.

An Upbeat Lesson

"A Ram Sam Sam" is a song from Morocco. Moroccan music is usually very rhythmic, with lots of percussion. You might hear this music played with hand drums, bells, and cymbals. What rhythm instruments do you hear in the recording of the song?

Sing "A Ram Sam Sam" and pat the strong beats.

CD 7–24

A Ram Sam Sam

Folk Song from Morocco

A ram sam sam, a ram sam sam,

Gu – li gu – li gu – li gu – li gu – li ram sam sam.

A ra – fi, a ra – fi,

Gu – li gu – li gu – li gu – li gu – li ram sam sam.

▲ Musicians from Morocco ▶

Add Accents!

Speak the words to "A Ram Sam Sam."
Say the upbeats softly. **Perform** the **accents**
that occur on the strong beats.

accent

An **accent** is used to give emphasis to a single note.

Parts to Play

Play this accompaniment to "A Ram Sam Sam."
Which part has accents marked on the strong beats?

Rondo-rama

This speech piece has three sections. Say the words to each section. Then **listen** to the recording and raise your hand each time you hear the **A** section.

A **rondo** is a musical form in which the **A** section repeats between two or more different sections.

CD 7–26

Bananas and Cream

Words by David McCord

Rhythmic Setting by Konnie Saliba

A

Ba - na - nas and cream, ba - na - nas and cream.

All we could say was ba - na - nas and cream.

B

We could - n't say fruit, We would - n't say cow. We

did - n't say su - gar, We don't say it now.

C

We for - got it was fruit, We for - got the old cow. We

ne - ver said su - gar, We on - ly said WOW!

Perform a Rondo

Here are some ways you can **perform** the sections of "Bananas and Cream."

- Speak the **A** section.

- Clap the rhythm of the **B** section.

- Whisper the **C** section.

What other ways can you think of?

Hear a Rondo

Listen to this rondo for harpsichord as you follow the listening map. How many different sections do you hear? How many times do you hear the **A** section?

CD 7–28
Country Dance

by Charles Dibdin

This piece was written for harpsichord. A harpsichord resembles a piano, but its strings are plucked instead of hammered.

Country Dance

Listening Map

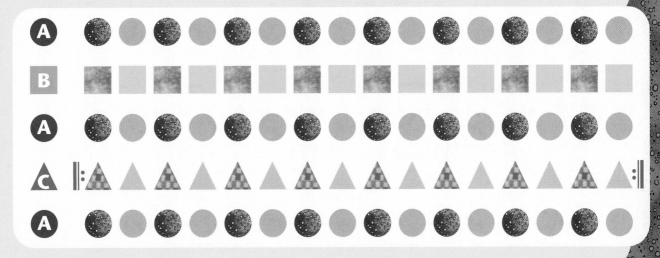

A Rondo Rap

"A Rondo for Lunch" also uses rondo form.
Perform this speech rondo.

CD 7–29

A RONDO FOR LUNCH

Words by Jack Prelutsky

Rhythmic Setting by Konnie Saliba

A
Rat for lunch, Rat for lunch, Yum, de-li-cious, Munch, munch, munch.

2nd time to Part C
Fine

One by one or by the bunch. Rat, oh rat, oh rat for lunch!

B
Rat, we love you steamed or stewed, Black-ened, broiled or bar-be-cued.

D. C.

Pick-led, poached or fried in fat, There is noth-in' like a rat!

C
In the ev'-ning we shall dine, On fil-let of por-cu-pine, Buz-zard,

D. C. al Fine

giz-zard, liz-ard chops. But for lunch, a rat is tops!

Rondo for Percussion

Clap the rhythm of each section of this rondo.
Perform the rondo on unpitched percussion instruments.

Create an introduction and a coda for your performance, using selected words from "A Rondo for Lunch."

A MICMAC MELODY

"Kwa-nu-te" is a gathering song of the Micmac of Nova Scotia, Canada. It is sung at the beginning of social events as people gather.

Listen to *"Kwa-nu-te."*

CD 7–31

KWA-NU-TE

Native American Song of the Micmac

O   kwa-nu - te ___ kwa-nu - te ___   kwa-nu - te ___ kwa-nu - tai

kwa-nu - te ___ kwa-nu - te ___   kwa-nu - te ___ kwa-nu - tai.

Kwa-nu - te ___ kwa-nu - te   Hey, kwa-nu - te ___ kwa-nu - te ___

kwa-nu - te ___ kwa-nu - tai.

What's the Tonal Center?

Look at the highlighted measure in *"Kwa-nu-te."*
This melody pattern occurs at the end of each phrase.
What is the last note of this pattern? When you find
the answer, you know the **tonal center** of this song.

The home tone of a song is also called the **tonal center**.

Play a Pattern

Pat this eighth note pattern as you **sing**
"Kwa-nu-te." Then sing the song again while
you **play** the pattern on drums.

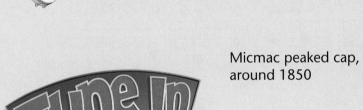

Micmac peaked cap, ▶
around 1850

Tune In

Between 1700
and 1900 European
settlers came to Nova
Scotia from Scotland and
Ireland. Their music
influenced the musicians
of the Micmac.

▼Micmac moccasins,
around 1840

A New Tonal Center

Listen for the tonal center as you **sing** this folk song from Kentucky.

CD 7–33

Pretty Saro

Folk Song from Kentucky

In some lone val - ley in a lone - some place,

Where the wild birds do whis - tle and their notes do in - crease,

Fare - well, pret - ty ___ Sa - ro, I bid you a - dieu,

But I'll dream of pret - ty Sa - ro where - ev - er I go.

Find the Tonal Center

Sing all of the pitches in "Pretty Saro" using pitch syllables and hand signs.

so_ı   la_ı   do   re   mi   so

You have sung songs that end on *do* and songs that end on *la*. On what pitch does "Pretty Saro" end? That pitch is the tonal center.

Show What You Know!

Sing each of these melodies with pitch syllables. What is the tonal center in each?

1. do

2. do

3. do

A Peddler's Song

Before supermarkets, people sometimes walked throughout the streets with carts to sell their goods. They would call out to get people's attention. "Hot Cross Buns" was a song a baker might have sung in England long ago.

Sing "Hot Cross Buns."

CD 7–38

Hot Cross Buns
(Version 1)

Folk Song from England

Hot cross buns, Hot cross buns,

One a - pen - ny, two a - pen - ny, Hot cross buns.

Hot cross buns, Hot cross buns,

If you have no daugh - ters, feed them to your sons.

What's the Difference?

Here is the first line of the song written two different ways.
Sing these two lines with pitch syllables. Use the same syllables
for both. How are the two lines different?

1. mi re do   mi re do

2. mi re do   mi re do

Letter Names for Pitches

You have been singing melodies with pitch syllables–*do, re, mi, so,* and *la.* These syllables can be anywhere on the staff. Musicians can also use letter names for pitches. Letter names stay in the same place on the staff. This "musical alphabet" uses letters from A to G to name pitches.

pitch syllables

letter names

mi   re   do
B   A   G

This is the musical alphabet.

C   D   E   F   G   A   B   C   D   E   F   G   A

treble clef

The G clef, or treble clef, curls around the second line of the staff, which is home to the letter name "G."

A Recorder Song

"Hot Cross Buns" (Version 1) is a perfect song for playing on your recorder. **Sing** the song with letter names. Then **play** the melody on your recorder.

More of the Same—or Is It?

Clap and say the rhythm syllables of this version of "Hot Cross Buns." How is the rhythm different from the first version of the song? What else is different about the two songs?

Listen to this song, and then **sing** it.

CD 7–43

Hot Cross Buns
(Version 2)

Folk Song from England

Hot cross buns! Hot cross buns!

One a pen - ny, two a pen - ny, Hot cross buns!

If you have no daugh - ters, Give them to your sons,

One a pen - ny, two a pen - ny, Hot cross buns!

Now **play** an accompaniment for this version of "Hot Cross Buns."

Recording Magic

Rick Bassett is a recording engineer. Each day he comes to work ready for new challenges.

Listen to Rick Bassett talk about his work.

CD 7–45
Interview with Rick Bassett (Part 1)

◀ Bassett records singers, instrumentalists, and narrators.

A recording engineer separates and then combines different tracks of a recording. Then he mixes all the parts.

Words to Know

track—a single vocal or instrumental line that is recorded separately

mix—to combine different tracks for a final recording

reverb—a recording effect that creates the resonance, or sound, of different sizes and types of rooms

equalizing—changing the color of a sound, making it brighter or darker

mixing board—a master control board where all tracks are mixed and equalized before final recording

▲ An engineer can take samples of sounds from different places and change them to get exactly what is needed for a recording.

Working with Sound

In this part of the interview, Bassett discusses how he can change sounds that he has recorded.

 CD 7–46

Interview with Rick Bassett (Part 2)

More Than a Melody

"A Small Job" is a song with a simple melody. When you hear a melody, you hear only one pitch at a time.

Sing "A Small Job" and learn the melody.

CD 7–47

A Small Job

Music by Jos Wuytack

Don't wor-ry if your job is small and your re-wards are few.

Re-mem-ber that the might-y oak was once a nut like you.

Tune In

The words of "A Small Job" are a proverb. A proverb is a wise, old saying.

Play While You Sing

Pat each of these patterns on your knees. Then **play** each of them on a mallet instrument.

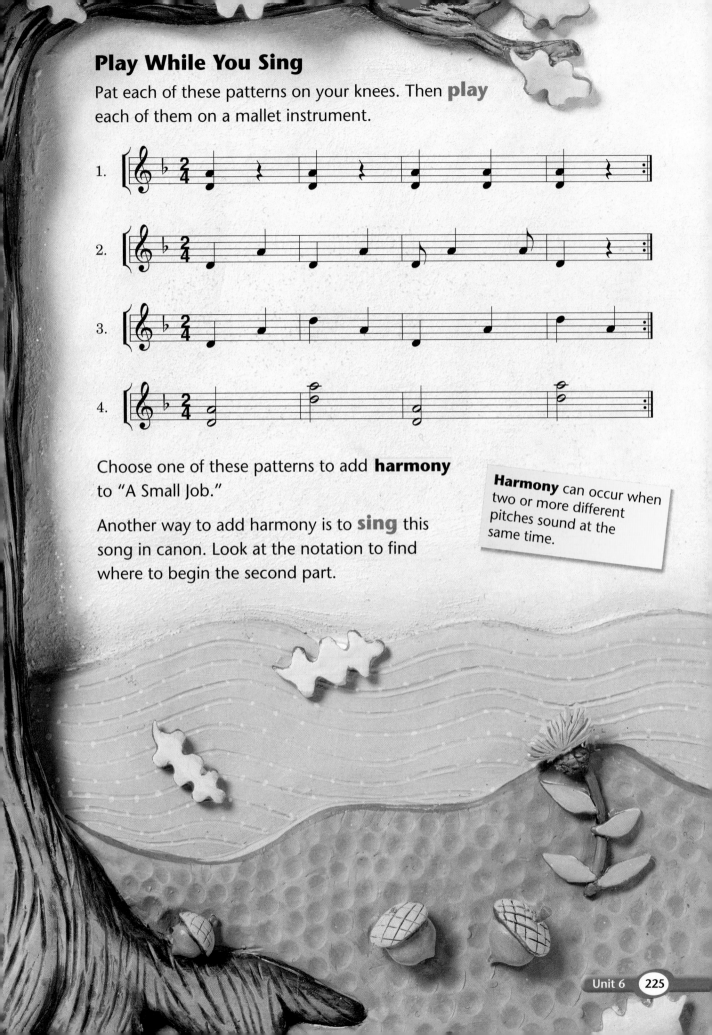

Choose one of these patterns to add **harmony** to "A Small Job."

Another way to add harmony is to **sing** this song in canon. Look at the notation to find where to begin the second part.

> **Harmony** can occur when two or more different pitches sound at the same time.

Two-Chord Harmonies

"Vamos a la mar" is a song about a family who fishes for its supper. **Sing** *"Vamos a la mar"* and act out the words.

CD 7–49

Vamos a la mar
(Let's Go to the Sea)

Folk Song from Guatemala

1. Va - mos   a   la   mar, ___ tun,   tun,
1. Let's   go   to   the   sea, ___ *tun,*   *tun,*

a   co - mer   pes - ca - do,   tun,   tun,
Hook   some   fish   and   fry   them,   *tun,*   *tun,*

bo - ca   co - lo - ra - da,   tun,   tun,
Mouth   as   red   as   ru - by,   *tun,*   *tun,*

fri - ti - to   y a - sa - do,   tun,   tun.
Bar - be - cue   or   fry   them,   *tun,*   *tun.*

2. Vamos a la mar, tun, tun,
   a comer pescado, tun, tun,
   fritito y asado, tun, tun,
   en sartén de palo, tun, tun.

2. Let's go to the sea, tun, tun,
   Catch a fish and grill it, tun, tun,
   Barbecue or fry it, tun, tun,
   In a wooden skillet, tun, tun.

Sea Harmony

You can add harmony to this song by accompanying it with **chords.**

Use resonator bells to **play** the chords as your class sings the song. Follow the highlighted chord symbols in the song to know when to change chords.

> A **chord** is three or more different pitches sounding at the same time.

▲ F chord

▲ C chord

Another Two-Chord Harmony

Here's another song that uses just two chords.
Listen to "Sweet Potatoes" and find the
chord markings in the music. Then **play** the
chords on the Autoharp as you **sing** the song.

◀ Autoharp

CD 7–53

Creole Folk Song

1. Soon as we all cook sweet po - ta - toes,
1. Soon as sup - per's done, Ma - ma hol - lers,

Sweet po - ta - toes, Sweet po - ta - toes,
Ma - ma hol - lers, Ma - ma hol - lers,

Soon as we all cook sweet po - ta - toes,
Soon as sup - per's done, Ma - ma hol - lers,

Eat 'em right straight up!
"Get a - long to bed!"

3. Soon's we touch our heads to the pillow, . . .
   Go to sleep right smart!

4. Soon's the rooster crow in the mornin', . . .
   Gotta wash our face!

Add a Layer

Play this bass metallophone part to add another layer of harmony to "Sweet Potatoes."

A Song in a Song

Listen to hear the "Sweet Potatoes" melody in this piano piece.

CD 7–55

Bamboula

by Louis Moreau Gottschalk

Gottschalk wrote *Bamboula* when he was only sixteen years old.

M·U·S·I·C M·A·K·E·R·S

Louis Moreau Gottschalk

Louis Moreau Gottschalk (1829–1869) was born in New Orleans. When he was only four years old, he could pick out tunes on the piano. At age thirteen, he went to study in Paris. He played his first recital there at sixteen. Gottschalk was one of the first American composers to incorporate folk songs into his music. He often used Creole folk melodies from Louisiana, where he grew up. He loved to travel throughout the world to play the piano and spread goodwill.

A World of Textures

Sing "He's Got the Whole World in His Hands," a very famous spiritual. What clapping pattern could you use as you **sing**?

CD 7–56
MIDI 21

He's Got the Whole World in His Hands

African American Spiritual

1. He's got the whole world __ in his hands, ___

He's got the whole world __ in his hands, ___

He's got the whole world __ in his hands, ___

He's got the whole world in his hands. _____

2. He's got the wind and rain in his hands, *(3 times)*
   He's got the whole world in his hands.

3. He's got-a you and me, brother, in his hands,
   He's got-a you and me, sister, in his hands,
   He's got-a you and me, brother, in his hands,
   He's got the whole world in his hands.

Adding Texture

Create an accompaniment to change the texture of "He's Got the Whole World in His Hands." Choose a nonpitched percussion instrument and **play** a short rhythm pattern as the class sings verse 1. Then **play** a rain stick and wind chimes for verse 2. Add temple blocks for verse 3.

Move to the Music

Add these movements as you sing.

whole world

wind

you and me, brother

Review, Assess,

What Do You Know?

1. Add the correct number of quarter notes to complete each measure.

2. Read each set of letter names below. What words do they spell?

3. Match each vocabulary word to its definition.

a. *crescendo* • gradually get softer

b. *decrescendo* • two or more pitches sound at the same time

c. rondo • gradually get louder

d. harmony • **A** section repeats between two or more different sections

What Do You Hear? 6

 CD 8–1

You will hear three selections. Point to the sign that describes the dynamics you hear.

1.

2.

3.

Perform, Create

What You Can Do

Play Chords

Look at the notation for "Sweet Potatoes" on page 228.

• Find the chords marked in the notation.

• Strum the chords on Autoharp as you sing.

• Create a one-measure rhythm pattern.

• Strum the chords, using your created rhythm, as the class sings the song.

Create a Rondo

You can create your own rondo.

• Create a four-line poem to use as an **A** section.

• Use body percussion, instruments, or movement to create a **B** and a **C** section.

• Perform your sections in rondo form.

PATHS TO Making Music

Can You Hear It?

Walt Whitman, an American poet, celebrated our country in a long poem called "I Hear America Singing." Here is part of his poem.

I Hear America Singing (excerpt)
by Walt Whitman

I hear America singing, the varied carols I hear. . .

Each singing what belongs to him or her and to none else.

Use Your Voice

Create your own poem about America.

• Make your poem at least four lines long.

• Practice reading your poem with feeling.

• Think about musical sounds you could use to accompany your poem.

• **Create** an accompaniment.

• **Perform** your poem with accompaniment.

Singing America

The United States is a country of many singers and many songs. What is your favorite American song?

Sing Across the Land

All across the United States, people enjoy singing together. Get ready to **sing** about the different people and places in our country.

CD 8–4

Sing, America, Sing!

Words and Music by Jill Gallina

Sing, A - mer - i - ca, sing! Lift up your voice __ in a song.

Sing, A - mer - i - ca, sing! Sing with a voice __ proud and strong.

With man-y fac - es from man-y pla - ces, A joy-ful mes-sage we bring,

A cel - e - bra - tion a - cross our na - tion, Let mer-ry mu - sic ring!

Sing, A - mer - i - ca, sing! Lift up your voice __ in a song.

Sing, A - mer - i - ca, sing!   Sing with a   voice __ proud and strong.

With songs we greet __ you, as   now we treat . you to a world of mel - o - dies.

So   lift up your voice __ in a   song,   and   soon all A - mer - i - ca

2nd time to Coda   *D. S. al Coda*

8   **9**

will   sing   a - long!

Sing,   A - mer - i - ca,   sing A - mer - i - ca,   sing!

BUILDING WITH SONG

Have you ever helped to build a doghouse, a tree house, or a birdhouse?

"Bling Blang" is a song about the sounds of building. Woody Guthrie, an American folksinger, wrote it for his children. **Listen** to the song, and then **sing** along.

BLING BLANG

CD 8–6

Words and Music by Woody Guthrie

VERSE

1. You get a ham-mer and I'll get a nail;

You catch a bird and I'll catch a snail;

You bring a board and I'll bring a saw, and

we'll build a house for the ba - by - o.

REFRAIN

F

Bling blang, ham - mer with my ham - mer,

C₇ ... **B♭** ... **F**

Zing - o zang - o, cut - ting with my saw.

2. I'll grab some mud and you grab some clay
So when it rains it won't wash away.
We'll build a house that'll be so strong,
The winds will sing my baby a song. *Refrain*

Building America

Listen to this recording by the folk group The Weavers. What do the singers want to build in this song?

CD 8–8
If I Had a Hammer

by Pete Seeger

This is a song that was written and sung during the civil rights movement of the 1960s.

MUSIC MAKERS

THE WEAVERS

The Weavers are known as the first successful folk group in mainstream popular music. They first sang together in 1948. The members were Pete Seeger, Lee Hayes, Fred Hellerman, Ronnie Gilbert, Erik Darling, and Frank Hamilton. Nearly all of the Weavers' records became hits. One of their best-known songs was "Goodnight Irene." It sold one million copies in 1950.

For fifteen years the Weavers traveled widely and made many recordings. In 1963 the group performed a final concert at Carnegie Hall in New York.

Singing on the Railroad

Singing can make work more fun. Workers on the Transcontinental Railway in the 1860s sang songs as they built railroad tracks across the United States.

Sing along with this famous railroad song.

CD 8–9

I've Been Working on the Railroad

Work Song from the United States

A *With a swing*

I've been work-ing on the rail - road, All the live-long day;

I've been work-ing on the rail - road, Just to pass the time a - way.

Don't you hear the whis-tle blow - ing? Rise up so ear-ly in the morn.

Don't you hear the cap-tain shout - ing: "Di - nah, blow your horn!"

B G

Di - nah, won't you blow, Di - nah won't you blow,

D₇   1. G   2. G

Di - nah, won't you blow your horn? _____ horn?

C G

Some - one's in the kitch - en with Di - nah,

G   D₇

Some-one's in the kitch - en, I know. _____

G   C   D₇   G

Some-one's in the kitch-en with Di - nah, Strum-min' on the old ban - jo.

G   3   3   D₇

Fee, fie, fid-dle-ee i o, fee, fie, fid-dle-ee i o, _____

slight ritard   *a tempo*

G   C   D₇   G

Fee, fie, fid-dle-ee i o, Strum-min' on the old ban - jo.

3

Track the Sounds

Look for the **A**, **B**, and **C** sections of the song. **Create** a rhythm ostinato for each section. **Perform** your train music.

Singing on the Sea

A sea shanty is a sailor's work song. One sailor sings the verses of the song. The other sailors join in on the refrain.

"Song of the Fishes" tells the story of a fisherman and some sea creatures. **Listen** to the verse and **sing** along with the refrain. Imagine what might happen if the fish took over the boat!

CD 8–11
MIDI 22

Song of the Fishes

Sea Shanty from the United States

1. Come all you bold fish-er-men, lis-ten to me,
   2. First comes the blue-fish a wag-ging his tail,

I'll sing you a song of the fish in the sea.
He comes up on deck and yells, "All hands make sail!"

Until I Saw the Sea

by Lilian Moore

Until I saw the sea
I did not know
that wind
could wrinkle water so.

I never knew
that sun
could splinter a whole sea
of blue.

Nor
did I know before,
a sea breathes in and out
upon a shore.

REFRAIN

Then blow ye winds west - er - ly, west - er - ly blow,

We're bound to the south - ward, so stead - y we go.

3. Next come the herrings
   with their little tails,
   They man sheets and halyards
   and set all the sails.

4. Next comes the porpoise,
   with his short snout,
   He jumps on the bridge
   and yells, "Ready, about!"

5. Then comes the mackerel,
   with his striped back,
   He flopped on the bridge
   and yelled, "Board the main tack!"

6. Up jumps the fisherman,
   stalwart and grim,
   And with his big net
   he scooped them all in.

Singing from the Heart

Music can help people express feelings. Spirituals are expressive folk songs, first sung by African Americans in the 1700s. **Listen** to "Peace Like a River." Think about the feelings expressed in this song as you **sing** along.

CD 8–13
MIDI 23

Peace Like a River

African American Spiritual

1. I've got peace like a riv-er, I've got peace like a riv-er,

I've got peace like a riv-er in my soul.

Signs of Peace

Learn to sign these words from "Peace Like a River." **Sing** the song as you **perform** the signs.

peace   *joy*   *love*

I've got peace like a riv-er, I've got peace like a riv-er,

I've got peace like a riv-er in my soul.

2. I've got joy like a fountain, *(2 times)*
   I've got joy like a fountain in my soul.
   I've got joy like a fountain, *(2 times)*
   I've got joy like a fountain in my soul.

3. I've got love like the ocean, *(2 times)*
   I've got love like the ocean in my soul.
   I've got love like the ocean, *(2 times)*
   I've got love like the ocean in my soul.

Spiritual Styles

Listen to these spirituals as you look at the pictures
of singers on these pages. What types of voices do you hear?
Do you hear men or women? Do you hear children or adults?

CD 8–15
Traveling Shoes

**Traditional African American
as performed by Sweet Honey in the Rock**

The women of Sweet Honey in the Rock have been
singing together for more than 25 years. Their
recordings include spirituals, children's songs,
freedom songs, and movie soundtracks.

CD 8–16
Ev'ry Time I Feel the Spirit

**Traditional African American
as performed by the Fisk Jubilee Singers**

The Fisk Jubilee Singers, from Fisk University in
Nashville, Tennessee, have been in existence since 1871.
They introduced spirituals to many people in
their concert tours around the world.

CD 8–17

He's Got the Whole World in His Hands

**Traditional African American
as performed by Marian Anderson**

Marian Anderson (1897–1993) sang all kinds of
music from spirituals to opera during her career.
Even though she faced discrimination, she
continued to sing and to break musical and
racial barriers.

Tune In

"What is important
is if we are striving . . .
to do the very best that is
in us to do."
—*Marian Anderson*

CD 8–18

Nobody Knows the Trouble I've Seen

**Traditional African American
as performed by the Boys Choir of Harlem**

The Boys Choir of Harlem was founded by Dr.
Walter J. Turnbull in 1968. The choir performs
spirituals, as well as other styles of music, including
jazz and classical. The Boys Choir has sung all over
the world.

Singing on the Trail

American cowboy songs are often stories about the challenges of cowboy life. **Sing** this cowboy song. What hardship is the cowboy singing about in "Texas Cowboy"? Why do cowboy songs have a steady beat?

CD 8–19

Texas Cowboy

Folk Song from Texas

1. Oh, I'm a Tex-as cow-boy, Far a-way from home,
2. I've worked up in the sand hills And down up-on the Platte,
3. But stay at home in Tex-as, Where work lasts the year a-round,

1.-2.

If I ev-er get back to Tex-as, I nev-er more will roam.
Where the cow-boys are all good fel-lows And cat-tle al-ways fat.
And you'll

3.

nev - er get con-sump-tion By sleep-ing on the ground.

Get with the Rhythm

Play this rhythm as you **sing** "Texas Cowboy."

Now play this rhythm as you sing the song.

Cowboy boots from the 1920s ▼

Music from the Trail

Listen to *Celebration*. What reminds you of a cowboy song in this recording?

CD 8–21
Celebration

from the orchestral suite *Billy the Kid* by Aaron Copland

This suite was originally written as a ballet about the life of the legendary American gunfighter, Billy the Kid.

▲ **A 1944 performance of the ballet *Billy the Kid* by the American Ballet Theatre**

Singing and Moving Together

Some music is for singing and moving. **Listen** for the word *jota* in "*La paloma blanca*." A *jota* is a dance. **Move** to feel the meter of the music. Then **sing** the song. Get ready to dance!

CD 8–22

La paloma blanca
(The White Dove)

English Words by Ruth De Cesare (adapted)

Folk Song from the Southwestern United States

VERSE

Yo soy tu pa - lo - ma blan - ca,
I'm your white dove, hear me sing - ing;

tú e - res mi pi - chón a - zul,
You're my pret - ty pi - geon blue.

a - rrí - ma - me tus plu - mi - tas,
Turn your beak to me, my dear one,

pa - ra ha - cer cu - rú, cu - cú.
And we'll sing "Coo - roo, coo - roo."

REFRAIN

F   **C₇**

A la jo - ta, jo - ta que bai - le, bo - ni - to,
To the *jo - ta, jo - ta* the fair ____ one danc - es,

C₇   **F**

A la jo - ta, jo - ta que bai - le él so - li - to,
To the *jo - ta, jo - ta* the fair ____ one danc - es,

F   **B♭**

A la jo - ta, jo - ta y con buen mo - di - to,
To the *jo - ta, jo - ta* the fair ____ one danc - es,

B♭   **F**   **C₇**   **F**

pa - ra ha - cer cu - rú, cu - cú.
"Coo - roo, coo - roo, coo - roo."

Play Along With the *jota*

Read the rhythm of these ostinatos. **Move** to show how you
will play each pattern. Then **play** these ostinatos to accompany
the verse of "*La paloma blanca*."

Songs of CELEBRATION

All around the United States, people sing songs on special occasions. Singing helps people celebrate traditions and customs. What songs do you sing on special occasions?

Listen to *"Inkpataya,"* a song sung by the Native American people of the Lakota nation. Sometimes this song is used for courting or for dancing at weddings.

 CD 8–26

Inkpataya

Native American Courting Song of the Lakota

Ink - pa - ta - ya   na - wa - zin   na - ya   si - na   ci - co - ze

ma - ya____   ma - ya____   le - ciya   ku   wa   na.

Listen to *"Inkpataya"* again. Tap with the beat as you listen. Does the tempo change or stay the same? Now **sing** the song.

 Take It to the Net Visit *www.sfsuccessnet.com* to learn more about Native American dance.

New Traditions

Listen to another version of *"Inkpataya."* This time the melody sounds like a lullaby. What instrument plays the melody?

CD 8–31
Wioste Olowan Inkpa Ta-Ya

**Native American Song
as performed by R. Carlos Nakai**

How is the melody played differently in this version?

M·U·S·I·C M·A·K·E·R·S

R. Carlos Nakai

R. Carlos Nakai (born 1946) is of Navajo and Ute heritage. He was born in Flagstaff, Arizona, and has played the music of his people since his youth. Nakai has also studied the melodies of the Plains and Woodlands people. He has developed his own style of playing the flute. It honors Native American tradition, but also includes new expressions. In 1992 Nakai became the second Native American to receive the Arizona Governor's Arts Award.

Songs of Honor

How many generations are alive in your family? Do you have grandparents or great-grandparents? Where do they live?

"O hal'lwe" is a song that honors the generations of women from the Nanticoke nation. The Nanticoke people lived in what is now Delaware.

Listen to *"O hal'lwe."* Tap lightly with the beat. Then **sing** the song.

CD 8–32

O hal'lwe

Native American Women's Dance of the Nanticoke

Yu no he yu ne la, yu no he yu ne la,

yu no he yu ne la yu no he, yu ne la.

O hal' - lwe O hal' - lwe O hal' - lwe O hal' - lwe

O hal' - lwe O hal' - lwe he yo heh!

Powwow Dance

Listen to *Round Dance,* and think about what it would be like to take part in a powwow, a tribal gathering. **Move** your feet to match the tempo.

CD 8–34
Round Dance

**Native American Dance
as performed by Northern Wind**

This round dance is accompanied by vigorous singing and the steady beat of drums.

▼ Native American powwow

Birds of Fire

from the Passamaquoddy People

We are the stars which sing.
We sing with our light.
We are the birds of fire,
We fly across the heaven.

Arts of the Arctic Circle

The Inuit people live in the very north of Alaska and Canada near the Arctic Circle. They have developed styles of music and art that are unique.

Arts Connection

◀ Inuit artists are especially skilled at carving. This carving is made of soapstone.

M·U·S·I·C M·A·K·E·R·S

Tudjaat

Madeline Allakariallal and Phoebe Atagotaaluk are cousins and members of the Inuit singing group **Tudjaat.** Their music combines traditional song forms with popular music styles. The song *Qiugaviit* is an example of the combined style. Allakariallal and Atagotaaluk are also experts at throat singing. As they sing, throat singers imitate the sounds of nature, such as the calls of geese and whales.

An Inuit Song

Trace the shape of the melody of *Qiugaviit* as you follow the listening map below. **Listen** for the sounds of the wind at the beginning and end of the song.

CD 8–35

Qiugaviit

Song of the Inuit (adapted) as performed by Tudjaat

In this song, an elder is scolding a younger man for going on a hunting trip without dressing warmly.

Qiugaviit

Listening Map

Songs of Nature

In Hawaii, nature is celebrated with songs, dances, and chants. **Sing** this song about the *hala* trees of Hawaii. As you sing, **move** to show the steady beat. Then use the chord symbols in the song and play an accompaniment on Autoharp.

CD 9–1

Nani wale na hala
(Lovely Hala Trees)

English Words by Alice Firgau

Folk Song from Hawaii

Na - ni wa - le na___ ha - la, E - a, e - a.
Love - ly are the ha - la trees, ___ E - a, e - a.

O___ Nau - e i - ke ka - i, E - a, e - a.
Sway - ing by the gen - tle seas. ___ E - a, e - a.

Ke___ o - ni a___ e - la E - a, e - a.
Near Ha - e - na ha - las grow, ___ E - a, e - a.

Pi - li ma - i Ha - e - na E - a, e - a.
In Na - u - e breez - es blow. ___ E - a, e - a.

Playing *Puili* Sticks

Puili [poo-EE-lee] sticks are traditional Hawaiian instruments. They are made of bamboo. The bamboo is slit in many places, so it makes a rattling sound. You can **play** *puili* sticks in different ways. Try tapping them together, or against your hand. They are often played while dancing.

Move to *"Nani wale na hala"* while you **play** the *puili* sticks.

More than ten thousand species of plants and animals live in the rainforests of the Hawaiian Islands.

singing at the GAME

Have you ever been to a major league baseball game? If so, you probably sang "Take Me Out to the Ball Game" during the seventh-inning stretch. Stand up and **sing** this song.

Major League Melody

Look for the steps and skips in the melody of "Take Me Out to the Ball Game." Here are some clues.

1.
2.
3.

Tune In

The first official baseball game was played in Hoboken, New Jersey, in 1846.

CD 9-6

Take Me Out
to the Ball Game

Words by Jack Norworth　　　　　　　　　　　　*Music by Albert von Tilzer*

Take　me　out　to　the　ball　game,

Take　me　out　with　the　crowd.

Buy　me　some pea-nuts and crack - er - jack,

I　don't care　if　I　ev - er　get back. Let　me

root,　　　root, root　for　the　home　team,　If

they　don't win　it's　a　shame,　　For　it's

one,　　　two,　　three strikes you're out　At　the

old　　　　　ball　　　　game.

Element: RHYTHM | **Skill: SINGING** | **Connection: SOCIAL STUDIES**

SONGS FOR THE FLAG

Songs that express pride in our country are called patriotic songs. "You're a Grand Old Flag" is a famous patriotic song.

Sing the song and tap the steady beat. Then tap and say the rhythm of the first line. Which measure has a syncopated rhythm?

CD 9–8
MIDI 24

YOU'RE A GRAND OLD FLAG

Words and Music by George M. Cohan

You're a grand old flag, you're a high - fly - ing flag;

And for - ev - er in peace may you wave;

You're the em - blem of the land I love,

The home of the free and the brave.

MUSIC MAKERS

George M. Cohan

George M. Cohan (1878–1942) was born in Rhode Island. As a boy, he performed in his family's vaudeville act. He became famous in 1904 as a character named Yankee Doodle Boy in the musical *Little Johnny Jones.* His song "The Yankee Doodle Boy" was first used in that musical. He wrote "Give My Regards to Broadway" and the World War I song "Over There." He also wrote about twenty plays and musicals.

Music Doodles

Listen for word clues that tell you this is a patriotic song.

CD 9–12
The Yankee Doodle Boy

by George M. Cohan

This song was used in several musicals other than *Little Johnny Jones.*

Ev - 'ry heart beats true un - der red, white, and blue,

Where there's nev - er a boast or brag;

But should auld ac - quaint - ance be for - got,

Keep your eye on the grand old flag.

The Small World of Music

All countries and people have special ways of using sounds to express themselves. Everyone has a special word for this—our word is *music.* You will hear many different kinds of music as you travel through this unit.

The different musical languages have their own ways of saying things. **Listen** to the bits of musical language on the recording. Can you match the music to the pictures?

CD 9–13
World Music Montage

Our World of Music

What if you could travel outside your own country in song? In music, it IS a small world.

Many Languages, One Song

What do we mean when we call the world "small"? What makes it seem smaller today than it was fifty years ago? **Sing** along with this well-known song.

It's a Small World

*Words and Music by Richard M. Sherman
and Robert B. Sherman*

VERSE

1. It's a world of laugh - ter, a world of tears,
2. There is just one moon and one gold - en sun,

It's a world of hopes and a world of fears.
And a smile means friend - ship to ev - 'ry one.

There's so much that we share, and it's time we're a - ware,
Though the moun - tains di - vide and the o - ceans are wide,

It's a small world af - ter all.
It's a small world af - ter all.

REFRAIN

Ab
It's a small world af - ter all,

Eb7
It's a small world af - ter all,

Ab
It's a small world af - ter all,

Db   Eb7   Ab
It's a small, small world.

Let's Play with RHYTHM

"*Al tambor*" is a song about drumming. **Listen** for the rhythm patterns as you **sing** the song.

CD 9–16
MIDI 25

Al tambor
(The Drum Song)

English Words by Mary Shamrock   *Children's Song from Panama*

Al tam-bor,   al tam-bor,   al tam-bor de la a - le - grí - a,
Won't you play,   won't you play,   won't you play the *tam-bor - ci - to?*

Yo quie - ro que tú me lle -ves   al tam-bor de la a - le - grí - a.
In time with the *tam-bor - ci - to*   we en - joy our life to -geth-er.

Ma - rí - a, oh, Ma - rí - a,   Ma - rí - a, a - mi - ga mí - a,
Ma - ri - a, oh, Ma - ri - a,   this drum is   a spe - cial trea-sure.

Yo quie - ro que tú me lle -ves   al tam - bor de la a - le - grí - a.
In   time with the *tam - bor - ci - to*   we   en - joy   our life   to - geth - er.

◀ The *caja* [KAH-hah] is a double-headed drum played with sticks.

The *repicador* [reh-PEEK-a-DOR] is a conga-type drum played with the hands. ▶

The *pujador* [poo-ha-DOR] is slightly larger and lower-sounding than the *repicador.* ▼

Drumming Is Fun!

Drums are important in Panama's traditional music. These three drums are often played together.

From your classroom instruments, select three different drums. **Play** the patterns below with the song. Play one part while your classmates play the others.

A Song of Welcoming

Long ago people came to New Zealand from the Pacific Islands in large canoes. They called themselves *Maori* [MOW-ree], which means "people of the land." *"Karangatia ra"* is a Maori song of welcome.

Clap the strong beats as you **sing** the song.

CD 9–20

Karangatia ra

Maori Action Song from New Zealand

Ka - ran - ga - ti - a ra —   Ka - ran - ga - ti - a ra —

Po - whi - ri - ti - a   ra   nga   i - wi   o   te   mo - tu

Ki   te - nei   ma - rae   ha - e - re   mai —

He   hui   a   ro - ha   mo   kou - tou   e   te - i - wi

Na - u   nei   te   a - ro - ha   me   te   ma - mae. —

Move to the Beat

This is a Maori action song. Use these actions to **move** to the music.

◀ *Karangatia ra*

◀ *haere mai*

me te ma-mae ▶

Arts Connection

◀ Maori wood carvings have different styles depending on where the carvers lived. Some carvings show wisdom. Others show bravery. Some carvings are meant to frighten evil away.

Arts of Cambodia

Classical dance is a treasured art form of Cambodia. It is the dance of the King's court. Children begin training before age 6 to develop the strength and flexibility needed to do this type of dance.

Listen to this classical music of Cambodia.

 CD 9–25
Mea haarit

Traditional from Cambodia

Mea haarit is an example of the classical music of the Cambodian royal courts. It is played during dance dramas.

Music of Cambodia

This popular Cambodian song is about the *sarika keo*. This native bird can be tamed and taught to say words!

CD 9–26
MIDI 26

English Words by David Eddleman

Sarika keo
(Bird Song)

Folk Song from Cambodia

1. Sa - ri - ka keo euy si ___ ey kang ___ kang? Ey sa - ri-yaing.
1. Oh, ___ ti - ny bird, tell me what do you eat? Ah sa - ri-yang.

Sa - ri - ka keo euy si ___ ey kang ___ kang? Ey sa - ri-yaing.
Oh, ___ ti - ny bird, tell me what do you eat? Ah sa - ri-yang.

Si phle dam - bang pra - choeuk ___ knea ___ leng.
A cac - tus fruit so ripe ___ and ___ sweet.

Euy keo keo ___ euy, euy keo keo ___ euy. ___
Oy koy koy ___ oy, oy koy koy ___ oy. ___

2. *Slap vea chakk kbach*
   moat vea thveu phleng.
   Ey sariyaing.
   (Repeat)
   Prachoeuk knea leng
   leu mek proeuksa.
   Euy keo keo euy,
   euy keo keo euy.

2. High in the sky
   you dance on the wing.
   Ah sariyang.
   (Repeat)
   High on a branch
   you fuss at everything!
   Oy koy koy oy,
   oy koy koy oy.

Frogs All Over

This counting song is well known all over the Szechuan [SEH-shwan] province of China. It is sung as a wish for peace.

Listen to hear how many phrases are in this song. Which ones are alike?

CD 9–30
MIDI 27

Shu ha mo
(Frogs)

English Words by Betty Warner Dietz and Thomas Choonbai Park

Folk Song from China

一　只　蛤　蟆　一　张　嘴
Yi　zhi　ha　ma　yi　zhang　zui
Each　frog　has　a　sin - gle　mouth,

两　只　眼　睛　四　条　腿
liang　zhi　yan　jing　si　tiao　tui
He　has　two　eyes　and　four　legs.

乒　乓　乒　乓　跳　下　水　呀
Pin　pong　pin　pong　tiao　xia＿＿　shui　ya
Ping　pong,　ping　pong,　count　them＿　with　me.

276

Playing with Frogs

Here is an accompaniment to **play** while you sing "*Shu ha mo.*" Then create a frog dance you can **move** to while you sing the song again.

Glockenspiel

Alto Xylophone

Bass Xylophone

蛤 蟆 不 吃 水　　太 平 ___ 年
ha　ma　bu　chi　shui　　tai　ping ___ nian
Dur - ing　time　of　peace,　frogs　do　not　drink.

荷 儿 梅 子 兮　　水 上 漂
he　er　mei　zi　xi　　shui　shang　piao.
Wa - ter　lil - ies　float　　on　the　pond.

Sunshine and Song

This Russian song expresses the total joy of a perfect day—the sun is shining, the sky is blue, a child and mother are having a good time, and they hope it can last forever.

CD 9–34

Pust' vsegda budet sonse
(May the Sun Shine Forever)

Russian Words by L. Oshanin
English Words by Alice Firgau

Music by A. Ostrovsky

Pust' 'vse - gda bu - det son - se,
May the sun shine for - ev - er,

Pust' 'vse - gda bu - det nye - ba,
May blue skies be for - ev - er,

Pust' 'vse - gda bu - det ma - ma,
May there ev - er be Ma - ma,

Pust' 'vse - gda bu - do ya! gda bu - do ya!
May there ev - er be me! ev - er be me!

The Shape of Sunshine

Look at the four lines of the song. **Compare** the rhythm patterns. Which ones are alike?

Dancing for Joy

In northern Russia, winter can be long and dark. When the snow melts and the sun brings back blue skies, everyone celebrates. In the old days, children would play singing and dancing games in the countryside to welcome the spring.

Follow the Form

Listen to this piece by a famous Russian composer. Follow the listening map to see the form.

CD 9–39
Trepak

**from *Nutcracker Suite for Orchestra*
by Piotr Ilyich Tchaikovsky**

Trepak is one of a group of dances from the ballet *The Nutcracker*.

Trepak
Listening Map

Piotr Ilyich Tchaikovsky

Piotr Ilyich Tchaikovsky [PYOH-ter IHL-yich chy-KOF-skee] was the first Russian composer whose music became well-known outside of Russia. His most famous works include *Symphony No. 5* and the ballets *Swan Lake* and *The Nutcracker.* He conducted his own music at the opening of Carnegie Hall in New York City in 1891.

Our World of Music

Take It to the Net Learn more about Tchaikovsky at *www.sfsuccessnet.com.*

HAPPY BIRTHDAY!

"*Mùbärak*" is sung for birthdays in Iran. Guests are invited to the home. This song and the dance that goes with it are part of their celebration. **Sing** this at your next birthday!

This song has two parts, but you sing the first part twice. What is the form of this piece?

CD 9–40

English Words by
Mary Shamrock

Mùbärak
(Happy Birthday)

Persian Birthday Song
As sung by Hooshang Bagheri

Mù - bä - rak, mù - bä - rak, ta - val - lu - det mù - bä - rak,
Hap-py day, hap-py day, here it is, your hap-py day.

mù - bä - rak, mù - bä - rak ta - val lu - det mù - bä - rak.
Hap-py day, hap-py day, here it is, your hap-py day.

La bat shä - di de let khush, chu gul pur khan-deh bä she
May this birth-day bring a year filled with all the best for you;

be - yä sham hä rä fot kun ke sad säl zen-deh bä she.
As you blow the can-dles out, may your spe - cial wish come true.

Everyone Loves a Birthday

Birthdays are special days all over the world. Look at these party pictures. What do they have in common?

◀ Germany

▲ Mexico

◀ Colombia

The Love of Country

This song expresses pride in the country of Israel. It speaks of joy in preparing the fields, planting the grain, and gathering the harvest.

Playing for Joy

Practice this ostinato. Then **play** it to accompany "*Artsa alinu.*"

Bass xylophone

Listen to find the steps, skips, and repeated pitches in the melody of *"Artsa alinu."* Then **sing** the song.

CD 10–1

Artsa alinu
(Come to the Land)

Folk Song from Israel

Ar - tsa   a - li - nu,   ar - tsa   a - li - nu,
Come to   the land   with joy   and with spir - it,

ar - tsa   a - li   -   nu.
Come to   our na - tive   land.

K'var   cha - rash - nu   v' - gam   za - ra - nu.
We   have plowed the   fields and   have plant - ed grain.

A - val   od   lo   ka - tsar   -   nu.
We'll reap   a   might - y   har   -   vest.

A - val   od   lo   ka - tsar   -   nu.
We'll reap   a   might - y   har   -   vest.

Rhythms of Africa

"*Sansaw akroma*" is a song from Ghana that goes with a stone-passing game. **Listen** for the syncopation as you **sing** the song.

CD 10–7

Sansaw akroma

Game Song from Ghana

San - saw a - kro - ma   ne   na wu o   ɔ - kye - kye   nko - kɔ - mba

1.

ɔ - seɔ   ke   yea dwu ma   ne   na wu o   ɔ - kye - kye   nko - kɔ - mba

2.

nko - kɔ - mba. E kyin e kyin e kyin kyin   A nan-tew a nan-tew a nan-tew

Ghana is a small country in West Africa. It has 72 languages, including an official sign language for the deaf.

Find the Form!

Listen to the song again. How many different sections do you hear? What is the form?

ɔ - seɔ ke yea dwu-ma   ne na＿ wu ̮o ＿   na je ＿ wu ̮o ＿   o

San - saw ̮a - kro - ma   ne nay wu ̮o   ɔ - kye - kye nko - kɔ - mba

ɔ - seɔ ke yea dwu-ma ne na wu ̮o ɔ - kye - kye nko - kɔ - mba.

◄ Drums from Ghana ►

Play a Rhythm Game

Play this game while you **sing** "Sansaw akroma" again.
Start with a small, smooth stone in front of you.

1. Pick up your stone and set it in front of the person on your right.

2. Pick up the stone in front of you and tap it once.

3. Set the stone in front of the person on your right.

4. Clap your hands.

Now, with your group, create your own stone-passing game. Try using two stones each. Share your ideas!

Listen to the Music

Listen to hear what instruments are included in this piece.

CD 10–10
Awakening

by Osei Tutu

This song is part of a Ghanaian music tradition called Highlife. It mixes traditional drum music with jazz from the United States.

▲ Highlife musicians from Ghana

Sing of the Irish

Have you ever heard of St. Patrick? He is a beloved person in Irish tradition. Why is he so popular? **Sing** the song and find an answer.

St. Patrick Was a Gentleman

CD 10–11
MIDI 28

Folk Song from Ireland

VERSE   Cm   B♭

St. Pat-rick was a gen-tle-man, He came of de-cent peo-ple,

Cm

In Dub-lin town he built a church, And on it put a stee-ple.

Cm   B♭

His fa-ther was a Call-a-ghan, His moth-er was a Bra-dy,

Sounds of Ireland

Traditional Irish music is performed and loved throughout the world. The Irish harp has a very special timbre. **Listen** for it in the recording.

◀ Irish harp

His aunt was an O-'Shaugh-ness - y, And his un - cle was a Gra - dy.

REFRAIN

Then suc-cess to bold St. Pat-rick's fist, He was a saint so clev - er,

He gave the snakes and toads a twist, And ban-ished them for - ev - er.

The Sound of the Irish

Listen to this Irish song. The first instrument you hear is a pennywhistle. The pennywhistle is a traditional Irish wind instrument. **Describe** its timbre.

CD 10–15
Roddy McCaulay

by The Clancy Brothers

The instruments in the accompaniment are added one by one—pennywhistle, guitar, and banjo.

M·U·S·I·C M·A·K·E·R·S

The Clancy Brothers

The Clancy Brothers moved to New York City from Ireland in the 1950s. They discovered a new way to perform traditional Irish songs that was appealing both to Irish Americans and to people who like folk music. They use guitar, banjo, pennywhistle, and energetic singing in their music.

Dance of the Irish

This is a dance similar to those you might see at an Irish
dance party, or *ceilidh* [KAY-lee]. Try these dance steps with
"St. Patrick Was a Gentleman."

The New-Found-Land

Newfoundland, a province in Canada, is well known for its fishing. This song is about a large port, called Bonavista, on the east side of the province. Fish are plentiful, so many people fish for a living. Clap to the beat as you sing.

CD 10–16

Bonavist' Harbour

Folk Song from Newfoundland

1. Oh,   there's   lots   of   fish   in Bon - a - vist' Har - bour,
2. Well,   now,   Un - cle George got   up   in   the morn - ing,

Lots   of   fish   right   in   a - round here.   Boys   and   girls   are
He   got up in   a   won - der - ful tear.   Ripped the seat   right

fish - ing to - geth - er, For - ty - five miles from Car - bon - ear.
out   of   his britch - es; Now __ he's got ne'er pair __   to wear.

A Lively Work Dance

This song is definitely meant for dancing! It even gives you some of the directions in the song. Move to this song as you sing.

REFRAIN

Oh, catch a - hold this one, catch a - hold that one,

Swing a - round this one, swing a - round she. Dance a - round this one,

dance a - round that one, Did - dle dum this one, did - dle dum dee.

Songs That Travel

These two songs came to Mexico and Puerto Rico from Spain. *"Sierra Morena"* is a game song. As you **listen**, perform a pat-clap pattern to the beat. Does this pattern fit the song? Why? Now **sing** the song and play the game.

CD 10–19

Sierra Morena

English Words by Cory Reeves

Folk Song from Mexico

De Sie - rra Mo - re - na que vien - en ba - jan - do
The gen - tle - man brings them from Sie - rra Mo - re - na,

cuat - ro pa - lo - mi - tas y un vie - jo a - rri - an - do.
four __ white __ doves sing - ing beau - ti - ful songs. __

The Wide Street of Three

Listen to this song that is sung in Puerto Rico. How will you change your pat-clap pattern to fit the song?

CD 10–23

La calle ancha
(The Wide Street)

English Words by Mary Shamrock

Folk Song from Puerto Rico

La ca - lle an - cha, cha, cha   de San Ber - nar - do,   do,   do
A-long the street wide, wide, wide   called San Ber - nar - do,   do,   do

Tie-ne u-na fuen - te,   te,   te   con cua - tro ca - ños, ños, ños.
There is   a foun - tain, tain,   tain   from which four streams flow, flow, flow.

2. Los cuatro caños, ños, ños
   dan agua hermosa, sa, sa
   Para los niños, ños, ños
   de Zaragoza, za, za.

2. In Zaragoza, za, za
   They shine and sparkle, kle, kle
   For all the children, dren, dren
   A gift so simple, ple, ple.

This song moves in three. What symbol in the music gives you a clue?

Playing in Three

Pick a partner and choose two different nonpitched percussion instruments . As you **sing** this song, **play** the first beat of each measure. Your partner then plays the other beats in each the measure on his or her own instrument. Can you **play** this same pattern while singing "Sierra Morena"? Why or why not?

How Low Can You Limbo?

Have you ever done the limbo? Here's your chance to try. You can take turns holding the limbo stick as you **move** to the music.

Can you invent other ways to go under the stick that will also be a challenge?

Music Under the Sun

Many different songs can accompany the limbo. The music is often played by a steel drum ensemble, or musical group. These instruments are made from oil barrels that are hammered into a drum shape. Hitting different areas of the drum sounds different pitches of the scale.

Dance the limbo to this steel drum ensemble recording of *Limbo Rock*.

CD 10–27
Limbo Rock

by William Stranger and Jon Sheldon

The limbo is a dance that was created in the Caribbean.

Fun and Games

**Music has energy.
It makes you want
to move!**

Sing, Dance, and Play

Music is used around the world for dancing and playing games. The songs in this unit will give you a chance to **move** in many different ways. Have a good time!

Children in Tobago like to sing this song while they clap in a circle. Learn to **sing** along with the song.

CD 10–28

Poco, Le' Me 'Lone

Folk Song from Tobago

Po - co, le' ___ me 'lone, le' me 'lone,

Me no mar - ry yet le' me 'lone.

When me mar - ry, o bell go ring,

When me mar - ry, o shell go blow.

Po - co, le' ___ me 'lone, le' me 'lone,

Me no mar - ry yet, le' me 'lone.

Tune In

Caribbean weddings are sometimes celebrated by ringing bells and blowing conch [kahnk] shell horns.

Who Goes First?

"*Jan ken pon*" is a Japanese game for making choices. In the United States, the game is called "Rock, Paper, Scissors." People play it to decide who starts a game or who is first in line. **Sing** and play the hand game.

CD 10–30
MIDI 29

Jan ken pon

English Words by Mary Shamrock

Collected by Mary Shamrock at the Nishi Hongwanji Temple Dharma School

おなかがすいたらグーグーグー
O - na - ka ga su - i - ta - ra goo goo goo,
When you have a hair - cut, scis - sors snip, snip, snip.

かみのけのびたらチョキチョキチョキ
Ka - mi - no - ke no - bi ta - ra cho - ki cho - ki cho - ki,
Hun - gry sto - machs of - ten make a grum - ble, grum - ble, grum - ble.

ほこりをはたいてパーパーパー
Ho - ko - ri wo ha - ta - i - te pa pa pa,
Wip - ing with a dust rag makes a slap, slap, slap.

(Spoken)

ジャンケンポンでダーチョキパー　ジャンケンポン
Jan ken pon de goo cho - ki pa.　*Jan ken pon!*
Snip, grumble, slap, now show me your hand!　Jan ken pon!

choki

pa

goo

Make Your Own Sounds

Create an accompaniment to
"Jan ken pon."

• Choose three different small percussion
  instruments for the words *goo, choki,* and *pa.*

• **Play** them when these words occur in the song.

• Use a wood block to play the steady beat.

• **Sing** the song as you play the accompaniment.

 Video Library See and hear how children from
other countries play singing games in *Singing Games.*

Catch a

Listen to the words of "Four White Horses." What do you think the *four white horses* might be? Why might a *shallow bay* of water be called a *ripe banana?*

CD 10–34

Four White Horses

Folk Song from the Caribbean

Four white hors - es on the riv - er,

Hey, hey, — hey, — up to - mor - row,

Up to - mor - row is a rain - y day.

Calypso Beat!

Calypso Clapping Game

You can limbo to this song, or play a clapping game.

A Note Challenge

How many measures of this song can you find that have only one pitch in them? What is the letter name of this pitch? **Play** this note on your recorder.

Come on up ___ to the shal - low bay.

Shal - low bay ___ is a ripe ba - na - na,

Up to - mor - row is a rain - y day.

Play the Wichita Way!

Hand games are played by many Native Americans. Game days are social occasions for people of all ages. Learn to **sing** these songs of the Wichita.

CD 10–36

Wichita Hand Game
Song 1

Game Song of the Wichita as sung by Stuart Owings

Hya ya ho we hya ya ho we hya ya ho we ya-o ya-o ho

CD 10–38

Wichita Hand Game
Song 2

Game Song of the Wichita as sung by Stuart Owings

Ya ____ we ha ya we ya ____ we ha

ya ____ we ha ya we ya ____ we ha ya we

Play the Game

Learn to play this game. Here's what you need.

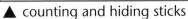

▲ counting and hiding sticks

▲ feather

▲ drum

Form two teams and sit facing each other. The "guesser" guesses in which hand the "hider" hides the short, marked stick. The team that guesses right five times wins!

Sounds of Brazil

"Ah, eu entrei na roda" is a game song from Brazil.

Listen to the song. How does the tempo change?

Sing the song before you learn the game.

CD 10–40
MIDI 30

Ah, eu entrei na roda
(I Came to Try This Game)

Circle Game from Brazil

Ah, eu en-trei na ro - da, pa-ra ver co-mo se dan-ça.
I came to try this game. __ I came to see the peo-ple danc-ing.

Ah, eu en-trei na con-tra dan-ça, Ah, eu nao sei dan-çar!
I came here to join the fun, but don't know how to dance!

La' vai uma, la' váo du-ás, la' váo três, pe-la ter-cei-ra,
There goes one and there goes two, there goes three, and on the third, There

la' se vai o meu a-mor de va-por p'ra ca-choi-e-ra!
goes my sweet-heart on a steam-boat down the riv-er to the sea.

Play an Accompaniment

Use resonator bells to **play** an accompaniment for *"Ah, eu entrei na roda."* **Play** these pitches on the steady beat.

Follow the chord symbols in the song notation to know when to change notes.

Arts Connection

Tucanos com Bananeíras by João Baptista Felga de Moraes ▼

Take It to the Net Go to *www.sfsuccessnet.com* to learn more about Brazilian music and dance.

Come and Try This Dance!

Move as you sing *"Ah, eu entrei na roda."*

- Hold hands in a circle.

- Move into the center for four beats, and then out for four beats.

- Repeat the in and out steps.

- Skip to your left.

Now comes the most fun! **Play** the accompaniment, but go faster and faster as you play. The rest of the class can **sing** and **move** to the song. Try to keep up!

Hear the Brazilian Beat

Listen to this exciting song in Afro-Brazilian style. Follow along with the listening map on the refrain of the song.

CD 10–45
Uma história de Ifá

by Ytthmar Tropicália and Rey Zulu as performed by Margareth Menezes

The layering of instruments and voices creates differing textures.

Uma história de Ifá

Listening Map

Refrain

Fun and Games

Lay It Down, Johnny Brown!

"Little Johnny Brown" is an African American game song. **Sing** the song and learn the motions.

Follow the Leader

Everyone enjoys being special. In this game you take turns being the leader. You can help each other by singing, clapping, and doing the motions with energy. Everyone gets a turn!

Tune In

The ring game is at least 100 years old. In this kind of game, the leader and group always take turns. This shows their support of one another.

Little Johnny Brown

CD 11–1

African American Singing Game

Em
Lit - tle John - ny Brown, lay your com - fort down,

Em **Am** **C₇** **Em**
Lit - tle John - ny Brown, lay your com - fort down.

Em
Now fold one cor - ner, John - ny Brown,___

Em **Em** **D** **Em**
Fold ___ the oth - er cor - ner, John - ny Brown. ___

Call **Em**
Fold the oth - er cor - ner, John - ny Brown,___
Give it to an - oth - er, John - ny Brown,___
Make a lit - tle mo - tion, John - ny Brown,___
Lope ___ like a buz - zard, John - ny Brown,___

Response **Em** **Em** **D** **Em** *Repeat 3 times*
Fold ___ the oth - er cor - ner, John - ny Brown. _
Give ___ it to an - oth - er, John - ny Brown. _
Make ___ a lit - tle mo - tion, John - ny Brown. _
Lope _____ like a buz - zard, John - ny Brown. _

'Round We Go!

This Polish folk song is written in meter in 3. Tap your foot on the strong beat of each measure as you **listen** to the song.

CD 11–3

Nie chcę cię znác
(Don't Want to Know You)

English Words by Mary Shamrock

Folk Song from Poland

Nie chcę cię, nie chcę cię, nie chcę cię znác.
Don't want to, don't want to, want to know you,

Chodź do mnie, chodź do mnie, rąez - kę mi daj.
Sor - ry, come back now, 'cause I real - ly do;

Pra - wą mi daj, le - wą mi daj.
Give me your right, give me your left,

Dance with a Friend

This dance is one of the first that Polish and Polish American children learn. The words of the song give cues for the dance steps.

I juz się na mnie nie gnie - waj.
Give me both hands and round we go.

Pra - wą mi daj, le - wą mi daj.
Give me your right, give me your left,

I juz się na mnie nie gnie - waj.
Thank you, my friend, now off we go.

Saying and Playing Hello

When you visit a country, you need to learn a few expressions for greeting people and being polite. Here is a speech piece that will get you started for a trip to Poland.

Create a percussion accompaniment to this piece. Choose different instruments for the Polish and English words. Speak the words while you **play** the accompaniment.

CD 11–9

Greetings

Words and Rhythmic Setting by Andrea Schafer

Cześć!   Hel - lo!   Dzień do - bry!   Good mor - ning!

Bar - dzo   mi - mi - lo.   Pleased to meet you.

Dzię ku - ję.   Thank you.   Pro - szę.   You're wel - come.

Prze - pra - szam.   Ex - cuse me.   Do - bra - noc.   Good night.

Polish Rhythms

Listen to this famous *mazurka* by the Polish composer, Frédéric Chopin.

CD 11–12

Mazurka, Opus 30, No. 3

by Frédéric Chopin

Traditionally, the *mazurka* is a Polish folk dance written in meter in 3. Chopin wrote 61 piano pieces based on this type of dance.

Tune In

The people of Warsaw, Poland, erected an enormous statue to honor Frédéric Chopin.

Music in the Morning

"I Wonder Where Maria's Gone" is a song that was written to play at dances. Learn to sing this folk song from Kentucky.

 CD 11–13

I WONDER WHERE MARIA'S GONE

Folk Song from Kentucky

1. I won - der where Ma - ri - a's gone,
2. She has come and I can't go, -

I won - der where Ma - ri - a's gone,
She has come and I can't go, -

I won - der where Ma - ri - a's gone,
She has come and I can't go,

So ear - ly in the morn - ing.
So ear - ly in the morn - ing.

3. Yonder she comes and "How do you do?"
   Yonder she comes and "How do you do?"
   Yonder she comes and "How do you do?"
   So early in the morning.

4. Shake her hand and wave on through,
   Shake her hand and wave on through,
   Shake her hand and wave on through,
   So early in the morning.

Dance in the Morning

Folk dancing is a very popular art form. You can **move** to a line dance while you **sing** "I Wonder Where Maria's Gone."

M·U·S·I·C M·A·K·E·R·S

GEORGE MARSHALL

George Marshall (born 1958) is a contradance caller and musician. A contradance is like a square dance, except it is done in lines instead of a square. First, Marshall teaches the dance steps with words. Then he plays concertina or *bodhran,* an Irish frame drum, with his band while the people dance. Sometimes he even calls the steps while he plays the music.

Marshall lives in Massachusetts, but he travels all over the country calling. He will work wherever there is a good wooden dance floor.

Sing a Silly Song!

Sometimes songs have words that don't make any sense, but they are fun to sing. Here's an example in Spanish. A *citrón* is a lemon. *Fandango* and *rondella* are dances. Dancing lemons are very silly!

CD 11–16
MIDI 31

Al citrón

Latino Nonsense Song from California

Al ci-trón de un fan-dan-go, San-go, San-go, Sa-ba-ré.

Sa-ba-ré de la ron-de-lla Con su tri-ki, tri-ki-trón.

Tune In

The *fandango* is a lively Spanish dance with meter in 3 that changes tempo.

320

I Was Walking in a Circle

by Jack Prelutsky

I was walking in a circle when I spied a piece of paper covered with a pretty picture colored yellow green and red as I picked it up I noticed that it also had some writing and I knew that I should read it this is what the writing said

Silly Games

Play a passing game while you **sing** *"Al citrón."*

Another Silly Song

Here's another song that is just for fun. The words for *"Al ánimo"* are nonsense, they go with the game for the song.

CD 11–19

Al ánimo

English Words by Alice Firgau

Folk Song from Spain

VERSE

Al á - ni-mo, al á - ni-mo, la fuen-te se rom-pió,
Al á - ni-mo, al á - ni-mo, The foun-tain has gone dry.

Al á - ni-mo, al á - ni-mo, man-dar-la a com-po - ner.
Al á - ni-mo, al á - ni-mo, Then fix it do not cry.

REFRAIN

¡Hu - rí, hu - rí, hu - rá! La rei - na va a pa - sar,
Hu - rí, hu - rí, hu - rá! The queen is pass-ing by,

¡Hu - rí, hu - rí, hu - rá! La rei - na va a pa - sar.
Hu - rí, hu - rí, hu - rá! The queen is pass-ing by.

2. Al ánimo, al ánimo,
   ¿con qué se hace el dinero?
   Al ánimo, al ánimo,
   con cáscara de huevo.

2. Al ánimo, al ánimo,
   From what is money made?
   Al ánimo, al ánimo,
   From cotton thread and braid.

Read a Silly Poem

Sometimes poetry is made from words and phrases that rhyme, but don't make much sense. This poem sneaks in a real meaning at the end—do you see it?

Going Places

by Dr. Fitzhugh Dodson

I'd fly to the moon
With a friendly racoon.
I'd ride a canoe
With a big kangaroo.
I'd take a sail
With any old whale.
And even eat peas
With chimpanzees.

BUT

I'd pack my trunk
If I met a skunk!

The Earth Is Our Home

There may be many beautiful planets in the universe, but to us the most beautiful is our home, the Earth.

Speak with expression as you recite this poem.

Valentine for Earth

by Frances M. Frost

Oh, it will be fine
To rocket through space
And see the reverse
Of the moon's dark face,

To travel to Saturn
Or Venus or Mars,
Or maybe discover
Some uncharted stars.

But do they have anything
Better than we?
Do you think, for instance,
They have a blue sea

For sailing and swimming?
Do planets have hills
With raspberry thickets
Where a song sparrow fills

The summer with music?
And do they have snow
To silver the roads
Where the school buses go?

Oh, I'm all for rockets
And worlds cold or hot.
But I'm wild in love
With the planet we've got!

This Beautiful Planet

Composers often write music about the Earth and its beauty. What do you love most about planet Earth?

The Big, Blue Marble

Imagine what it's like to look at Earth from space.
Astronauts sometimes call Earth the "big blue marble."
Sing about our beautiful planet.

Big Beautiful Planet

CD 11–23

Words and Music by Raffi

REFRAIN

There's a big beau-ti-ful plan-et in the sky, _____

And it's my home, _____ It's where I live.

You and man-y oth-ers live here too. _____

The earth is our home, _____ It's where we live. _____

Fine

Can You Cuckoo?

Many songs imitate the sounds of birds. **Listen** for the call of the cuckoo in this song. What instrument can you **play** to make the cuckoo sound?

CD 11–25

El mes de abril
(The Month of April)

Folk Song from Spain

I   F   C   F

El   mes de a - bril   lle - gó,   y el   cu - cu   ya   can - tó:
The month of   A - pril's here,   The   cuck-oo's song we   hear.

II

Cu - cú,   cu - cú,   el   cu - cu   ya   can - tó.
Cuck - oo,   cuck - oo,   The cuck-oo's song we   hear.

A Cuckoo Accompaniment

Play these accompaniments while you **sing** the song.

Glockenspiel

Alto Metallophone

Listen to this piece that was written almost three hundred years ago! Can you hear the call of the cuckoo?

CD 11–29

Le cou cou

by Louis-Claude Daquin

Many composers have used bird calls as inspiration for their music.

Tune In

When a bird is born, it already knows how to sing part of the song of its bird family.

Let Your Spirit Soar

Plovers are birds that live near the ocean. Feel the long phrases as you **sing** the song.

CD 11–30

Hama chi dori
(Plovers)

Words by Meishu Kashima

*School Song from Japan
Music by Ryutaro Hirota*

あ　　　　お　　　　い　　　　つ　　　　き　　　　よ　　　　の
Aa　　　　o　　　　ii　　　　tsu　　　　ki　　　　yo　　　　no
When　　the　　blue _____　moon　　-　　light

は　　　　ま　　　　べ_____　に　　　　は _____
ha　　　　ma　　　　be _____　ni　　　　wa _____
shines　　up　-　on _____　the　　shore, _____

お　　　　や　　　　を　　　　さ　　　　が　　　　し　　　　て
oh　　　　ya　　　　wo　　　　sa　　　　ga　　　　shi　　　　te
From　　a　-　mong　　the　　gleam　-　ing　　waves

な_____　く　　　　と　　　　り　　　　が_____
na _____　ku　　　　to　　　　ri　　　　ga. _____
ba　　-　　by　　plov　-　ers　　soar, _____

Haiku for You

Haiku [hy-KOO] is a three-line Japanese poem that is often about the seasons and nature. Haiku lets the reader imagine a scene.

Looking for the Mother Birds

by Issa, Haiku Master Poet

Warbler, wipe your feet neatly, if you please, but not on the plum petals!

な	み	の	く	に	か	ら
Na	*mi*	*no*	*ku*	*ni*	*ka*	*ra*
Look	- ing	for	the	moth	- er	birds,

う	ま	れ_____	で	る_____
U	*ma*	*re_____*	*de*	*ru_____*
how	they	fly _____	and	cry, _____

ぬ	れ	た	つ	ば	さ	の
Nu	*re*	*ta*	*tsu*	*ba*	*sa*	*no*
Wa	- ter	bathed, _____		bright _____		wings,

ぎ	ん	の	い	ろ_____
ghi	*_n*	*no*	*i*	*ro._____*
sil	- ver	- y	the	sky. _____

Music in Bloom

TEXAS

Each state in the U.S.A. has an official state flower. For Texas, it's the bluebonnet. Why do you think it has this name? Before you **listen** to the song, look at the five lines of the song. Where do you think the phrases end? Why? How many phrases are there?

CD 11–34

Bluebonnets of Texas

Words and Music by Beatrice P. Krone

1. Blue - bon - nets of Tex - as, they bloom in the spring.
2. Though far o'er the wide world a - roam - ing I go,

A car - pet of blue that will make your heart sing.
I'll dream of the land where the blue - bon - nets grow.

I love dear old Tex - as in sum - mer and fall,
Though oth - ers find beau - ty on moun - tain or sea,

A Legend in Bloom

A Native American legend explains how this flower originated. There are many versions of the story. Your teacher will choose someone to read the legend. Why did the Great Spirits create the bluebonnets? What is the moral of this story?

Playing in Bloom

Play the two parts below. Then **sing** the song while you and a classmate play the parts.

A Rabbit Tale

Storytelling is an important part of Native American tradition. **Listen** to this story of the Mohawk people.

CD 11–36
The Rabbit Dance

Traditional Native American

Long ago, some hunters went out looking for game. When they got to an open field, what they saw amazed them. A giant rabbit, so big that it looked like a small bear, was standing alone. The hunters hid and watched. What they saw was remarkable. The large rabbit tapped a rhythm with its foot and, lo and behold, many rabbits appeared and started to dance.

Listen to the recording of *The Rabbit Dance* to find out why the rabbits were dancing.

Poetry Plus Percussion

Create a percussion accompaniment for "A Song of Greatness." **Play** your percussion parts as other students read the poem aloud.

A Song of Greatness

**from *My Song Is Beautiful*
A Chippewa Song**
Translated by Mary Austin

When I hear the old men
Telling of heroes,
Telling of great deeds
Of ancient days,
When I hear them telling,
Then I think within me
I too am one of these.

When I hear the people
Praising great ones,
Then I know that I too
Shall be esteemed,
I too when my time comes
Shall do mightily.

Canta, el sapito

Sometimes you can hear the sound of a small insect or animal but cannot see it. **Listen** to "*El sapito.*" Where do you think the toad is?

CD 11–37
MIDI 32

El sapito
(The Little Toad)

Words by Jose Sebastian Tallón
English Words courtesy of CP Language Institute

Music by Wilbur Alpírez Quesada

Na - die sa - be don - de vi - ve, en la ca - sa no lo vió,
No one knows just where the toad lives. We can't find him in the house.

pe - ro to - dos lo es - cu - cha - mos, el sa - pi - to glo, glo, glo.
But we know we all can hear it. Lit - tle toad, sing *glo, glo, glo.*

Vi - vi - rá en la chi - me - ne - a? Vi - ve o - cul - to en u - na flor?
May - be liv - ing in the chim - ney, May - be hid - den in a rose.

Don - de can - ta cuan - do llue - ve? el sa - pi - to glo.
When it rains where does the toad sing? Lit - tle toad, sing *glo.*

"Toad-ally" Musical

Sing *"El sapito."* Which two lines of the melody are exactly alike? Which lines have the most skips in the melody?

Now **play** these ostinatos with the song. Then add another instrument to make a "toad sound."

Our Mr. Toad

by David McCord

Our Mr. Toad
Has a nice abode
Under the first front step.
When it rains he's cool
In a secret pool
Where the water goes
    drip
    drop
    drep

Our Mr. Toad
Will avoid the road
He's a private-cellar man.
And it's not much fun
In the broiling sun
When you *have* a good
    ten
    tone
    tan.

Our Mr. Toad
Has a kind of code
That tells him the coast
    is clear.
Then away he'll hop
With a stop, stop, stop
When the dusk draws
    nigh
    no
    near.

Beautiful Day, Beautiful Song

Some days are so beautiful they make you feel like singing!
Make a list of all the beautiful things in this song. Then
sing the song in your most beautiful voice.

CD 11–41

It's a Beautiful Day

Words and Music by Greg Scelsa

See the sun   shin-ing in the win-dow,   time to start a   new _ day. _

Can't you hear the song-birds sing-in'?   Got-ta sing out loud and say _

That it's   a   beau-ti-ful day _   for run-nin' in the sun,   a
Yes, it's a

beau-ti-ful   day _   that's just _   be-gun, _____   a

beau-ti-ful day   to   do what I wan-na do, _   uh-huh! ___

Yes, it's a beau-ti-ful day __ just to be a - live, __ a

beau-ti-ful day, _ so glad _ that I've _ got a beau-ti-ful day _ and

I'd like to share it with you. _____

Look a - round, there's a world of beau - ty

from the moun - tains to the sea, ____

And there's a won - der 'round _ ev - 'ry cor - ner

a - wait - ing there for you and me. ____

The Rhythm of Earth

What will happen to the Earth if we don't take care of it?

"Look Out for Mother Earth" is a song about our environment. It is in the style of a rap. Rap music began in the 1970s in New York City. The words are spoken over a rhythm accompaniment.

Write a Rap

Think of some words that have to do with saving our planet. Then use some of your words to **create** a rhythm pattern. **Play** the pattern on an instrument. Here are some examples.

1. Re - use   and   re - cy - cle

2. Save   the   Earth.

Speak Out for Mother Earth

Listen to the rhythms of the piece as you follow along with the words. **Sing** the refrain when you can.

 CD 11–43

 Look Out for Mother Earth

Words and Music by Bryan Louiselle

VERSES

1. We gotta tell you, Mom,
      we gotta tell you, Dad,
   That we don't have
      ev'rything you had.
   We're not talkin' money
      or a life of ease;
   We're talkin' water, (Clean water!)
      clean water and trees.
   Hey, what's up with all the smoke
      from the factories?
   (to Refrain)

2. There's stuff goin' on
      that you can't even see:
   There's a hole in the sky
      where a hole shouldn't be.
   We're talking ozone. (Ozone?) Definitely.
   And if we don't cut back on C. F. C.s,
   We're gonna all need sunblock
      a thousand and three.
   (to Refrain)

3. Ev'ry fish and mammal,
      ev'ry insect and bird
   Makes a contribution,
      is a voice to be heard.
   Won't you hear the voice?
      Won't you feel the pain?
   They're sayin' oil spills!
      (Oil spills?) and acid rain.
   And everything else we're puttin'
      down the drain! Here we go again!
   (to Refrain)

4. Hey, teacher,
      won't you help us plot a strategy?
   Plan a plan for the planet.
      Plant a flower or tree.
   Promote ecological diversity.
   Not just for you, not just for me.
   It's for the kids
      in the next (Next!) century.
   (to Refrain)

REFRAIN

1. You got-ta look out, (Look out!) look out for the plan-et.

You got-ta look out, (Look out!) Look out for Moth - er Earth.

We Love the Earth

The world is full of beautiful places. Where is your favorite place?
What do you see there? Think about this place as you **sing**
"The World We Love."

CD 12–1

The World We Love

Words and Music by Raffi and Michael Creber

REFRAIN

do

Here's   to   the   world   we   love,

Blue   skies   and   po - nies   and   child - ren   at   play,

Earth   be - low,   stars   a - bove,

God   bless   it   ev - 'ry - day.

Melody Moves

How does the melody of "The World We Love" move, by step or by skip? **Move** to follow the shape of the melody.

VERSE

C   Em   F   C

1. Mist - cov - ered   moun - tains   that   wel - come   the   sun,
2. Praise   to   the   farm - er   out   work - in'   the   fields,

C G_7

Buds   on   the   branch - es,   morn - ings   be - gun,
Seed - ling   to   har - vest,   food   for   our   meals,

Am   Em   F   C

Dew - drops   and   blue - birds   just   start - ing   to   sing
Ma - mas   and   pa - pas,   and   hearts   filled   with   love

F G_7 C   *D.C. al Fine*

Praise   for   the   brand   new   day.
For   each   and   ev - 'ry   day.

3.   Here's to the rivers that run wild and free,
The pull of the tides, the rush of the sea,
Gold crimson sunsets to color our dreams
In each and ev'ry day.   *Refrain*

CELEBRATE NATURE!

There is so much beauty in nature. People sing about the sky, the trees, the flowers, and the wind. They write poems about the moon, the stars, and the ocean. They dance and celebrate the splendor that they see all around them.

Sing "A Song of One." Take turns singing the verses.

CD 12–3

A Song of One

Words and Music by John Forster and Tom Chapin

1. Sing a song of one, one for the yel-low sun,

the yel-low sun that's shin-ing down on ev-'ry-one.

2. Sing a song of two, two for the sky of blue, *(to Verse 2 ending)*
3. Sing a song of three, three for the red-wood tree, *(to Verse 3 ending)*
4. Sing a song of four, four for the sand-y shore, *(to Verse 4 ending)*
5. Sing a song of five, five for the things a-live, *(to Verse 5 ending)*

344

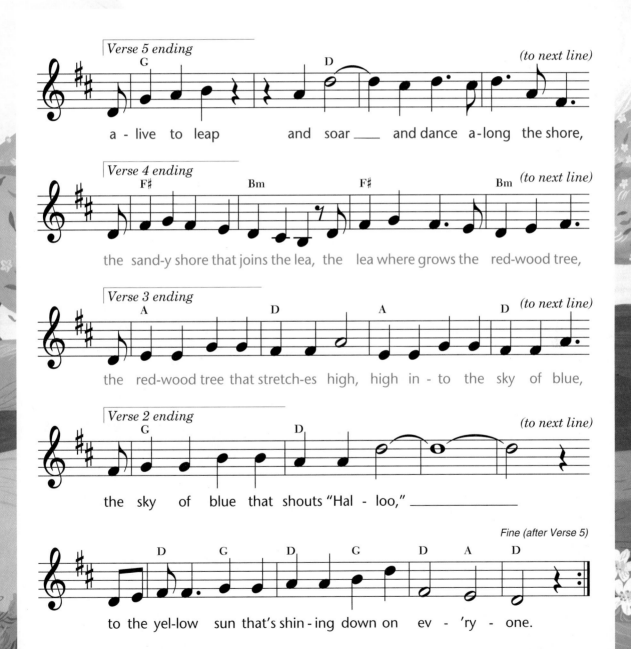

Verse 5 ending

G   D   *(to next line)*

a - live to leap   and soar ___ and dance a - long the shore,

Verse 4 ending

F♯   Bm   F♯   Bm *(to next line)*

the sand-y shore that joins the lea, the lea where grows the red-wood tree,

Verse 3 ending

A   D   A   D *(to next line)*

the red-wood tree that stretch-es high, high in - to the sky of blue,

Verse 2 ending

G   D   *(to next line)*

the sky of blue that shouts "Hal - loo," _____

Fine (after Verse 5)

D   G   D   G   D   A   D

to the yel-low sun that's shin - ing down on ev - 'ry - one.

Celebrate the Night

Listen to this poem as it is read. Imagine the
scenes that the poet is describing.

CD 12–5

The Song of the Night

by Leslie D. Perkins

I dance to the tune
of the stars and the moon.
I dance to the song of the night.

I dance to the strains
of a cricket's refrain.
I dance to the fireflies' light.

I dance to the breeze
and the whispering trees.
I dance to the meteor's flight.

I dance to the beat
of the summertime heat.
I dance to the pulse of the night.

Express Yourself

Decide how you would like to read this poem. Think about different ways you can express the meaning of the words. Here are some suggestions.

• Vary the dynamics of each verse.

• Change the tempo of each verse.

• Choose some of the words and lines to repeat.

• Say the first lines of each verse one after the other.

• Experiment with saying the repeated words. Try using accents and different tempos and dynamic levels.

Create a Sound Symphony

Create sound effects to accompany your reading of "The Song of the Night."

• What instrument can you use to create a song of the night?

• What images or words can you express through sound effects?

Create a Movement Symphony

Can the moon dance? Can stars, crickets, or trees dance? If they could, what would it look like? **Move** like this yourself and **create** a night dance!

Story Time!

Stories and tales can serve many purposes. Some tell of events that happened many years ago. Others end with a moral. Some are told just to make us laugh!

Songs are often stories that are set to music. Sometimes it is easier to remember a story that you can sing. What songs do you know that tell a story?

Tell a Story

Make up a short story with two classmates. One of you can say the story, one can create movements, and one can play an ostinato. Together you can also create scenery by illustrating the story.

Perform the story for the class.

Tuneful Tales

Sometimes a song
can help to tell a story,
and sometimes the
song IS the story.

Tunes to Tell

"Sing Your Story" tells us different ways we can share stories and tales. **Sing** along with the recording.

CD 12–6

Sing Your Story

Words and Music by Bryan Louiselle

VERSE

1. All a - round the world, in ev - 'ry time and place,
2. Fa - bles to ___ in - spire, or fair - y tales for fun,

Stor - ies help _ us learn a - bout the hu - man race.
Par - a - bles _ that teach a tale for ev - 'ry - one,

Leg - ends that _ we share, ad - ven - tures we _ en - joy,
Stor - ies from _ the past and ev - 'ry dis - tant land

Bring us to - geth - er, ev - 'ry girl and _ boy,
Bring us to - geth - er, help us un - der - stand,

Bring us to - geth - er, ev - 'ry girl and _ boy. (So, come a - long now!)
Bring us to - geth - er, help us un - der - stand. (So, ev - 'ry - bod - y!)

350

SING DON GATO'S TALE

You know that there are different kinds of songs, like spirituals, dance songs, and echo songs. "Don Gato" is a **ballad**. **Listen** for the surprise ending!

> A **ballad** is a song that tells a story.

CD 12–8

Don Gato

English Words by Margaret Marks

Folk Song from Mexico

1. El se - ñor Don Ga - to es - ta - ba
1. Oh, Se - ñor Don Ga - to was a cat,

sen - ta - di - to en el te - ja - do
On a high, red roof Don Ga - to sat.

cuan - do le vi - nie - ron car - tas, mi a - rra - miau,
He went there to read a let - ter, meow, meow, meow,

cuan - do le vi - nie - ron car - tas, mi a - rra - miau,
Where the read - ing light was bet - ter, meow, meow, meow,

si que - rí - a ser ca - sa - do. ____
'Twas a love note for Don Ga - to! ____

The Pattern in Rhythm

Look at the rhythm of each phrase of the song.
Which phrases have the same rhythm?

2. *Con una gatita blanca,*
   sobrina de un gato pardo,
   que no la había más linda, . . .
   que no la había más linda, . . .
   en las casas de aquel barrio.

3. *Don Gato con la alegría,*
   se ha caído del tejado;
   ha roto siete costillas, . . .
   ha roto siete costillas, . . .
   las dos orejas y el rabo.

4. *A visitarlo venían,*
   médicos y cirujanos;
   todos dicen que se muere, . . .
   todos dicen que se muere, . . .
   que Don Gato está muy malo.

5. *El gatito ya se ha muerto,*
   ya se ha muerto el buen Don Gato;
   a enterrar ya se lo llevan, . . .
   a enterrar ya se lo llevan, . . .
   todos los gatos llorando.

6. *Cuando pasaba el entierro,*
   por la plaza del pescado,
   al olor de las sardinas, . . .
   al olor de las sardinas, . . .
   Don Gato ha resucitado.

2. "I adore you!" wrote the lady cat,
   Who was fluffy, white, and nice and fat.
   There was not a sweeter kitty, . . .
   In the country or the city, . . .
   And she said she'd wed Don Gato!

3. Oh, Don Gato jumped so happily,
   He fell off the roof and broke his knee,
   Broke his ribs and all his whiskers, . . .
   And his little solar plexus, . . .
   "¡Ay caramba!" cried Don Gato!

4. Then the doctors all came on the run
   Just to see if something could be done,
   And they held a consultation, . . .
   About how to save their patient, . . .
   How to save Señor Don Gato!

5. But in spite of ev'rything they tried,
   Poor Señor Don Gato up and died,
   Oh, it wasn't very merry, . . .
   Going to the cemetery, . . .
   For the ending of Don Gato!

6. When the funeral passed the market square,
   Such a smell of fish was in the air,
   Though his burial was slated, . . .
   He became re-animated! . . .
   He came back to life, Don Gato!

Listen to an Animal Beat

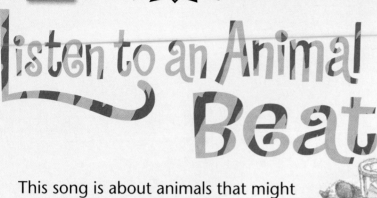

This song is about animals that might worry you. What did the composer do to add suspense to the song?

 CD 12–12

If a Tiger Calls

Words and Music by Elizabeth Gilpatrick

1. If a ti - ger calls in the mid - dle of the night
2. If a li - on calls in the mid - dle of the day
3. If a croco - dile calls and in - vites you out to dine,

and in - vites you out for a lit - tle ev' - ning bite,
and in - vites you out for an af - ter - noon buf - fet,
tell him, "Thank you, _____ next De - cem - ber would be fine."

Last verse to Coda

do be war - y, for zo - ol - o - gists have shown that the
do be war - y, for zo - ol - o - gists have shown that the
And be war - y, for zo - ol - o - gists will state that the

ti - ger lies on the phone.
li - on lies on the phone.

croc - o - dile lies, the croc - o - dile lies,

Fm

the croc - o - dile lies in wait!

Play Body Percussion

- Speak the words of the song.
- Snap your fingers twice for the word *tiger*.
- Clap your hands twice for the word *lion*.
- Pat your knees three times for the word *crocodile*.
- Brush your hands together for the words *in wait*.
- Be sure you use a quiet, "sinister-sounding" voice!

The Panther
(excerpt)

by Ogden Nash

If called by a panther,

Don't anther!

Playing with Tigers!

Play this accompaniment with the first four lines of "If a Tiger Calls." **Create** a new verse about another animal.

Arts Connection

▲ *Surprised!* by Henri Rousseau [aw(n)-REE roo-SOH] (1844–1910)

This painting is one of several famous jungle scenes by Rousseau. What do you think surprised the tiger?

Beastly Music

The lion is a very stately animal. It has padded feet and walks softly. **Listen** to *The Royal March of the Lion*. What instrument plays the lion's melody?

CD 12–14

The Royal March of the Lion

from *Carnival of the Animals*
by Camille Saint-Saëns

Carnival of the Animals uses orchestral instruments to create images of animals through sound.

MUSIC MAKERS

Camille Saint-Saëns

Camille Saint-Saëns [kah-MEEL sa(n) SAW(n)] (1835–1921) was born in Paris, France. He composed his first piano piece when he was three years old. An excellent pianist and organist, he performed in many countries. He also composed music for piano, orchestra, and voice. *Carnival of the Animals* was a piece he wrote just for fun. Now it is one of his most famous compositions.

Tuneful Tales

Tiny Boat Notes

This folk song from Latin America tells a story about a boat so tiny that it could not even sail.

CD 12–15
MIDI 33

El barquito
(The Tiny Boat)

English Words by Kim Williams

Folk Song from Latin America

Ha - bía u - na vez un bar - co chi - qui - ti - co,
Oh, there was once a boat so ve - ry ti - ny,

Ha - bía u - na vez un bar - co chi - qui - ti - co,
Oh, there was once a boat so ve - ry ti - ny,

Ha - bía u - na vez un bar - co chi - qui - ti - co,
Oh, there was once a boat so ve - ry ti - ny,

Que no po - dí - a, que no po - dí - a, que no po -
So ve - ry ti - ny, so ve - ry ti - ny, it could not

dí - a na - ve - gar.   *Pa - sa - ron u - na, dos, tres,*
e - ven sail a - way.   It sat for one, two, three, four,

Count and Sing

Before you **sing** the song, practice counting from one to seven in Spanish: *uno, dos, tres, cuatro, cinco, seis, siete.*

cua - tro, cin - co, seis, sie - te se - ma - nas.
five, six, sev - en weeks there in the har - bor.

Pa - sa - ron u - na, dos, tres, cua - tro, cin - co,
It sat for one, two, three, four, five, six, sev - en

seis, sie - te se - ma - nas.   Pa - sa - ron
weeks there in the har - bor.   It sat for

u - na, dos, tres, cua - tro, cin - co, seis, sie - te se -
one, two, three, four, five, six, sev - en weeks there in the

ma - nas.   Y el bar - qui - to, que no po -
har - bor.   It was so ti - ny, so ve - ry

dí - a, que no po - dí - a na - ve - gar.
ti - ny, it could not e - ven sail a - way.

Rhythm Search

Look for these two rhythm patterns in *"El barquito."*

1.
2.

Now clap pattern 1, and pat pattern 2. Then **perform** the rhythm patterns as they occur in the song.

Move to the Rhythms

For the first half of the song, **move** with a partner. Using the pattern below, step, then clap your partner's hands. Then move in a circle for eight beats.

step   step   step   step   step   clap clap clap

Signing Away

Here's another way to perform this song. **Sing** the song, and use these hand signs.

uno
(one)

dos
(two)

tres
(three)

cuatro
(four)

cinco
(five)

seis
(six)

Listen for the percussion solo in this Latin American music.

CD 12–19
Picadillo

by Tito Puente

Tito Puente [PWEHN-tay] made more than one hundred recordings of Latin American and swing music.

siete
(seven)

Tuneful Tales

Sounds of South America

The people of Chile, a country in South America, have sung this song and danced to it for hundreds of years. The violin, called *el rabel*, was brought to Chile by the Spanish almost 500 years ago.

This song has two sections, **A** and **B**. **Listen** to the recording. Raise your hand when you hear the **B** section.

CD 12–20

El rabel
(The Violin)

English Words by Patricia Shehan Campbell

Folk Song from Chile

> El ra - bel pa - ra ser fi - no ha de ser de ver - de pi - no,
> The *ra - bel* it is so fine and it's made of fresh green pine,

> la vi - hue - la d(e) du - ra he - bra y el se - dal de mu - la ne - gra,
> The *vi - hue - la's* ___ stur - dy shell you know it holds the strings so well.

> la vi - hue - la d(e) du - ra he - bra y el se - dal de mu - la ne - gra.
> The *vi - hue - la's* ___ stur - dy shell you know it holds the strings so well.

Move Along
Move to show the form.

B

G   C   D   G

An - da mo - re - ni - ta   re - co - je e - se   pa - ñue - lo.
Let   the   girl ___ go   there and   pick   up   the hand - ker - chief.

G   C   D   G

Mi - ra que es de   se - da y   lo a - rras - tras por   el   sue - lo.
Silk - en   hand - ker - chief: she's   drag - ging   it   on   the   floor.

LESSON 5

Element: TEXTURE/HARMONY **Skill: PLAYING** **Connection: CULTURE**

Layers to Learn

This is a story from West Africa. Many cultures use stories to teach children the rules they should follow. **Listen** to "Zomo the Rabbit." What do you think is the lesson in this story?

CD 12–24
Zomo the Rabbit

A Trickster Tale from West Africa

Zomo the Rabbit is one of many tricksters found in West African folk tales. Like all tricksters, clever Zomo outwits his larger foes.

In this story, Zomo wants to gain wisdom. The story begins with Zomo asking Sky God how he could become wise. Sky God tells Zomo that he must complete three almost impossible tasks. The story explains these tasks and how Zomo succeeds in his quest for wisdom.

Play with the Story

Learn to **play** this line of music.

Now **play** this line to add another layer.

Create a thicker texture by adding this line of music.

Tell Your Story

Retell the story of Zomo, using your own words.
Play these ostinatos together as a musical theme between the sections of the story.

Video Library Watch *Storytelling* to learn about different ways to tell a story through music and movement.

Sing with a Spider

Music in movies is used to help tell the story. "We've Got Lots in Common" is from a movie you may know. **Sing** along with the animals in this song.

CD 12–25

We've Got Lots in Common

from *Charlotte's Web*

Words and Music by Richard M. Sherman
and Robert B. Sherman

1. Oh, we've got lots in com-mon where it real - ly counts,
2., 3. 'Cause we've got

Where it real - ly counts, we've got large a - mounts.

What we look like does - n't count an ounce,

We've got lots in com-mon where it real - ly counts.

(Wilbur) 2. You've

Another Song from a Story

Listen to *Circle of Life,* a song from another movie. What do the words tell you?

CD 12–27

Circle of Life

**from *The Lion King*
by Elton John and Tim Rice**

This song is about appreciating the mystery of life.

(Wilbur) 1. You've got feath-ers, I've got skin, but both our out-sides hold us in.
got a beak and I've a snout, but both of us can sniff a-bout.

(Cow) I've got hooves, you've got webbed feet, but we both stand up to eat,
(Horse) You'll say "quack" and I'll say "neigh," but we're talk-ing ei-ther way,

real - ly counts. _____

(Charlotte) 3. You're born to swim and me to spin,
but we all love this world we're in.
We share the sun, the earth, the sky
and that's the reason why
We've all got . . . (D.S.)

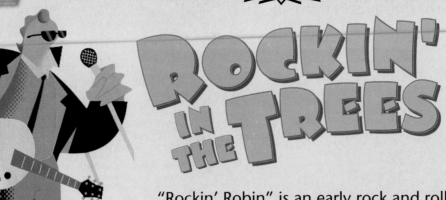

"Rockin' Robin" is an early rock and roll song. Imagine how it might feel to be a bird who could dance *and* fly!

Sing the song. For every verse, create a different steady-beat dance.

CD 13–1

Rockin' Robin

Swing style

Words and Music by Leon René

1., 3. He   rocks   in the tree - top   all the day   long,
2. Ev'ry   lit - tle swal - low,   ev - 'ry chicka - dee,

Hop - pin' and a - bop - pin' and a - sing - in' his   song.
Ev - 'ry lit - tle bird __ in the tall   oak   tree. The

All   the   lit - tle birds   on   Jay - bird Street
wise __   old __ owl,   the   big   black   crow,

Love   to   hear the rob - in   go "Tweet, tweet, tweet,"
Flap __   their __   wings, __ singin' "Go,   bird,   go,"

REFRAIN

Rock-in' Rob-in,   Rock-in' Rob-in.

Blow, Rock-in' Rob-in, 'cause we're real-ly gon-na rock to-night. _

1.

2., 3.

A pret-ty lit-tle ra-ven at the bird band-stand

Taught him how to do the bop and it was grand. They

start-ed go-in' stead-y, and bless my soul, He

out-bopped the buz-zard and the o-ri-ole.

Take It to the Net Go to *www.sfsuccessnet.com*
to learn more about rock and roll music.

Tuneful Tales

Fats Domino

Antoine "Fats" Domino (born 1928) was one of the first rock and roll stars. He came from a musical family and as a child played piano and sang. In 1950 he had a hit song called "The Fat Man." That song became a nickname for him. In the 1950s he hit the national music scene with his own piano style. He has influenced many rock and roll singers. In 1986, Fats Domino took his place in the Rock and Roll Hall of Fame.

Tune In

During the 1950s Fats Domino sold more records than any rock star except Elvis Presley.

Walk and Rock

Listen to Fats Domino perform *Walkin' to New Orleans*.
Follow the shape of the melody on the listening map.
What instruments do you recognize?

CD 13–3

Walkin' to New Orleans

by Domino/Bartholomew/Guidry

This song is written in rock 'n' roll style. How would you
describe its tempo?

Walkin' to New Orleans
Listening Map

Tuneful Tales

Dancin' with a Bully!

"Wooly Bully" is a popular dance song from the 1960s. **Listen** to the Sam the Sham & The Pharaohs recording of *Wooly Bully* and follow the lyrics on the next page.

CD 13–4
Wooly Bully

Sam the Sham & The Pharaohs

Domingo Samudio was also known as "Sam the Sham." He blended garage-style rock with Latin sounds when he wrote "Wooly Bully."

Who are the main characters in this story? After you listen to the verses of "Wooly Bully," **describe** what happens to the characters. Listen to the recording again. What is different between the second and third verses? **Listen** to the refrain. What are the only two words sung during the refrain?

Now **sing** "Wooly Bully."

Wooly Bully

Words and Music by Domingo Samudio

VERSE

1. Mat-ty told Hat-ty   A-bout the thing she saw _

Had two big horns   And a wool-y jaw.

REFRAIN

Wool - y   Bul - ly _____   Wool - y

Bul - ly   Wool-y Bul-ly   Wool-y

Bul - ly   Wool - y   Bul - ly.

2. Hatty told Matty
   Let's don't take no chance,
   Let's not be L 7
   Come and learn to dance
   Refrain

3. Matty told Hatty
   That's the thing to do,
   Get yo' someone really
   To pull the wool with you—
   Refrain

Tune In

In the 1960s pop music culture, a wooly animal-like vest was often worn by performers. This was known as a wooly bully vest!

Tuneful Tales

Unit 11 **373**

Celebrations!

Sing "Let's Celebrate," a song for any holiday.

Holidays to Share

All through the year, there's something to celebrate!

To-ge-ther we'll dance and __ sing now, you and me.

As our voi - ces ____ ring,

to - ge - ther what joy we'll __ bring.

To - ge - ther we'll dance and ____ sing

D. C. al Coda ⊕ *Coda*

in har - mo - ny. have such fun! __

Sing and Move to Celebrate

Holidays are a time for special songs and dances. **Move** to the beat as you **listen** to "Go With the Music and Sing." Then **sing** and celebrate as you move to the music.

Go With the Music and Sing

CD 13–9

Words and Music by Rhonda Macken

Go with the mu - sic when you feel your bod - y mov - in',

Go with the mu - sic and sing. ___

Move to the rhy - thm with a tap - pin' and a clap - pin',

Come on and make those walls ring. ___

Play to Celebrate

Read and clap the ostinatos below. **Play** them to accompany "Go With the Music and Sing."

Songs that you'll sing right out and songs that are qui - et.

Some to sing __ by day and some by night, So

go with the mu - sic and sing. __

Go with the mu - sic and sing. _ Let's sing! _

United in Peace

Celebration songs are used for many reasons. *"Hevenu shalom aleichem"* is a song that celebrates peace. **Move** to show same and different phrases as you **sing** the song.

CD 13-11

Hevenu shalom aleichem
(We Come to Greet You in Peace)

Hebrew Folk Song

He - ve - nu sha - lom a - lei - chem, He - ve - nu
We come to greet you in peace, ___ We come to

sha - lom a - lei - chem, He - ve - nu sha - lom a -
greet you in peace, ___ We come to greet ___ you in

lei - chem, He - ve - nu sha - lom, sha - lom,
peace, ___ We come to greet you, greet you,

1.

2.

sha - lom a - lei - chem. He - ve - nu sha - lom a - lei - chem.
greet ___ you in peace. We come to greet ___ you in peace.

▲ United Nations Building, New York City

Show Your Colors!

In 1945, fifty-one countries joined together to form the United Nations. The goal of the United Nations is peace through cooperation. Today more than 180 countries belong to the United Nations. Each nation has a flag flying at the U.N.

Listen to *Common Ground*. It celebrates the environment. The composer was honored for his contribution to environmental causes.

CD 13–15

Common Ground

**from *Concert for the Earth*
by Ivan Lins
as performed by
the Paul Winter Consort**

Common Ground was recorded live at the United Nations Assembly Hall.

Paul Winter playing ▶
a soprano saxophone

Pumpkin Time!

Have you ever been in a pumpkin patch? If so, you know that pumpkins grow on vines. They can be used for pies, decorations, or jack-o-lanterns. **Sing** this pumpkin patch song.

CD 13–16

In the Pumpkin Patch

Words and Music by Elizabeth Gilpatrick

1. When I grew up in the pump - kin patch,

I sat in the sun all day.

I grew 'til I was gold and round,

Then I heard a lit - tle sun - beam say:

2. "Roll around, little pumpkin in the pumpkin patch;
Oh, tumble and turn and sway.
Roll around in the grasses and the weeds and the thatch,
Oh, spin and roll and play.

3. "But when the sun is sinking low
And shadows steal the light,
Hurry back to your home in the garden row;
Curl up in your vines so tight."

Pumpkin Rhythms

Read the rhythms of "In the Pumpkin Patch." Tap and say the rhythm for each phrase of the song.

Read this poem. Then **create** ostinatos to accompany it.

Pumpkin Poem

Author Unknown

One day I found two pumpkin seeds.

I planted one and pulled the weeds.

It sprouted roots and a big, long vine.

A pumpkin grew; I called it mine.

The pumpkin was quite round and fat.

(I really am quite proud of that.)

But there is something I'll admit

That has me worried just a bit.

I ate the other seed, you see.

Now will it grow inside of me?

(I'm so relieved since I have found

That pumpkins only grow in the ground!)

A Tricky Song

On Halloween, you might see people dressed in unusual costumes. Or you might wear an unusual costume yourself! **Listen** to "Halloween Is a Very Unusual Night." What unusual things are mentioned in this song?

CD 13–18

Halloween Is a Very Unusual Night

Words and Music by Ned Ginsburg

1. There's on-ly one night like this all year,
2. Drop ___ your fears and off you go,

On-ly one night when spi-rits ap - pear;
Join ___ the tra - veling cos - tume show. ___

An eve - ning meant to be spent out - side,
Grab your sack and at - tack the street,

Yes, it's Hal - lo - ween, and you can - not hide.
But you bet - ter start to ___ trick - or - treat.

Catch a Rhythm

Clap the rhythm patterns of the refrain as you **sing** the song. Then **create** your own rhythm ostinatos to accompany the song.

REFRAIN

When the ghosts come out,   and the gob-lins creep,

and the skel-e-tons rat-tle.   How could an - y - bod - y sleep?

And the mon-sters march,   while the witch-es take flight.

Yes, Hal - lo-ween is a ver-y un-u - su-al night!

Yes, Hal - lo-ween is a ver-y un-u - su-al night!

Head for Thanksgiving

Thanksgiving is a time for getting together with family and friends. **Sing** this traditional song about Thanksgiving.

 CD 13–20

Over the River and Through the Wood

Words by Lydia Maria Child   *Traditional*

1. O - ver the riv - er and through the wood,

To Grand - fa - ther's house we go; _____

The horse knows the way to car - ry the sleigh

Through the white and drift - ed snow. _____

O - ver the riv - er and through the wood,

Oh, how the wind does blow! _____

Arts Connection

Freedom from Want
by Norman Rockwell (1894–1978)
This painting is one of a series
called *The Four Freedoms.* ▶
Rockwell was famous for painting
pictures of everyday American life.

It stings the toes and bites the nose

As o- ver the ground we go.

2. Over the river and through the wood,
   Trot fast, my dapple gray!
   Spring over the ground like a
       hunting hound,
   For this is Thanksgiving Day!

   Over the river and through the wood,
   Now Grandmother's face I spy!
   Hurrah for the fun! Is the
       pudding done?
   Hurrah for the pumpkin pie!

Holidays to Share

Winter Weather Music

In some parts of the world, winter is so cold, you can see your breath in the air! What happens when winter arrives in your town? **Sing** this winter song in unison. Then sing it in canon.

Knock No More

CD 13–22
MIDI 34

Words and Music by Elizabeth Gilpatrick

When Old Man Win-ter ___ comes knock-ing at your door,

he'll nip your fin - gers ___ and freeze you to the core.

Knock! Knock! Can't come in! Knock no more!

Play in Winter

Play these ostinatos to accompany "Knock No More." What happens to the texture of the song when each ostinato is added?

Create Winter Music

Read "Dragon Smoke," then **create** a rhythm ostinato to go with it.

Dragon Smoke

by Lilian Moore

Breathe and blow
white clouds
    with every puff.

It's cold today
    cold enough
to see your breath.

Huff!
    Breathe dragon smoke
      today!

Sing for Chanukah

A dreydl is a spinning top that is used in Chanukah games. There are four symbols on the dreydl—*nun, gimel, hay*, and *shin*.

Listen to "Chanukah Games." What do the four symbols mean in the game?

Holiday Melody

Look at the song. Find a place where the melody moves by skip. Find a place where the melody moves by step. Which measures are the same?

Sing "Chanukah Games." Sing the octaves smoothly.

Chanukah Games

Words by Rose C. Engel and Judith M. Berman

Music by Judith M. Berman

VERSE

1. Cha - nu - kah's the time for games. Read - y, now be - gin!
2. Round and round the drey - dl goes, See it hop and run.

Spin your drey - dl, let it go, Ev - 'ry - one join in.
When at last it stops on *nun,* Priz - es? Not a one.

Spin your drey - dl, let it go, Ev - 'ry - one join in!
When at last it stops on *nun,* Priz - es? Not a one.

REFRAIN

Nun and *gi - mel, hay* and *shin,* Los - er, win - ner, spin and spin!

3. In a circle, dreydl, turn, turn and slowly sway.
   If you stop on *gimel* now, I win all—Hooray!
   If you stop on *gimel* now, I win all—Hooray! *Refrain*

4. Funny little dreydl top, how you make me laugh!
   But if now you stop on *hay,* I take only half!
   But if now you stop on *hay,* I take only half! *Refrain*

5. Whirling, twirling, dreydl, go, on one foot you dance;
   Shin says I must put one in and take another chance!
   Shin says I must put one in and take another chance! *Refrain*

Eight Days to Celebrate

Keep the beat while you **sing** *"Hanuka, Hanuka."*

CD 13–26

Hanuka, Hanuka
Words and Music by Flory Jagoda

VERSE

1. Ha - nu - ka, Ha - nu - ka, O - cho __ di - yas di fe - li - si - ta.
1. Ha - nu - ka, Ha - nu - ka, Eight days of joy __ for __ Ha - nu - ka.

Ha - nu - ka, Ha - nu - ka, O - cho __ di - yas di fe - li - si - ta.
Ha - nu - ka, Ha - nu - ka, Eight days of joy __ for __ Ha - nu - ka.

REFRAIN

lai lai lai lai lai lai lai lai lai lai lai lai lai lai lai lai lai

lai lai lai lai lai lai lai lai lai

lai lai lai lai lai lai lai lai lai lai lai lai lai

The Way to Celebrate

Chanukah celebrations include singing, dancing, and playing games. One candle is lit on each of the eight nights of Chanukah.

Holiday Listening

Describe the melody of this funny Chanukah song.

The word *Chanukah* can be spelled in different ways, but it always means "dedication."

CD 13–30
The Dreydl Song

Traditional Hebrew

You can make up your own verses to this song about making dreydls.

2. *Hanuka, Hanuka,*
   Ocho diyas de kantar.
   Hanuka, Hanuka,
   Ocho diyas de kantar.
   Refrain

3. *Hanuka, Hanuka,*
   Ocho diyas de bailar.
   Hanuka, Hanuka,
   Ocho diyas de bailar.
   Refrain

4. *Hanuka, Hanuka,*
   Ocho diyas de guzar.
   Hanuka, Hanuka,
   Ocho diyas de guzar.
   Refrain

2. Hanuka, Hanuka,
   Eight days of singing for Hanuka.
   Everyone sing, let voices ring,
   Eight days of singing for Hanuka.
   Refrain

3. Hanuka, Hanuka,
   Eight days of dancing for Hanuka.
   Raise arms high, let feet fly,
   Eight days of dancing for Hanuka.
   Refrain

4. Hanuka, Hanuka,
   Eight happy days of Hanuka.
   Play, dance, and sing, let voices ring,
   Eight happy days of Hanuka.
   Refrain

Holidays to Share

Sing the Songs of Christmas

"Children, Go Where I Send Thee" is a Christmas spiritual. Create a way to **move** for each verse of this add-on song.

CD 14–1

Children, Go Where I Send Thee

African American Spiritual

1. Chil-dren, go where I send thee; How shall I send thee?

I will send thee one by one. ___

Well, one was the lit-tle bit-ty ba-by, ___

Wrapped in swad-dling cloth-ing, ___

Ly-ing in the man-ger. ___

Born, born, _____ Born in Beth-le-hem. ___

A Mountaintop Christmas

Listen for the verse and refrain in another Christmas spiritual.

CD 14–3

Go, Tell It on the Mountain

Traditional African American

This version is sung by the Booker T. Washington Singers.

2. Children, go where I send thee;
    How shall I send thee?
    I will send thee two by two.
    Well, two was the Paul and Silas,
    One was the little bitty baby,
    Wrapped in swaddling clothing,
    Lying in the manger.
    Born, born,
    Born in Bethlehem.

3. . . . I will send thee three by three.
    Well, three was the three men riding,
    Two was the Paul and Silas, . . .

4. . . . I will send thee four by four.
    Well, four was the four come a-knocking at the door,
    Three was the three men riding, . . .

5. . . . I will send thee five by five.
    Well, five was the Gospel preachers,
    Four was the four come a-knocking at the door, . . .

6. . . . I will send thee six by six.
    Well, six was the six that couldn't be fixed,
    Five was the Gospel preachers, . . .

7. . . . I will send thee seven by seven.
    Well, seven was the seven who went to heaven,
    Six was the six that couldn't be fixed, . . .

8. . . . I will send thee eight by eight.
    Well, eight was the eight who stood by the gate,
    Seven was the seven who went to heaven, . . .

9. . . . I will send thee nine by nine.
    Well, nine was the nine who saw the sign,
    Eight was the eight who stood by the gate, . . .

10. . . . I will send thee ten by ten.
    Well, ten was the Ten Commandments,
    Nine was the nine who saw the sign, . . .

A Quiet Style

Some of the songs of Christmas
have a quiet and calm style.
Listen to the style of "Silent
Night." **Move** to show the
phrases as you **sing** the song.

CD 14–4

Silent Night

Words by Joseph Mohr   *Music by Franz Gruber*

Si - lent night, ho - ly night, All   is calm,   all   is bright

Round yon Vir - gin Mo-ther and child. Ho - ly In-fant so ten-der and mild,

Sleep in heav-en-ly   peace, _   Sleep _ in heav-en-ly   peace. _

Celebrate in Style

How do you like to celebrate? **Sing** "We Wish You a Merry Christmas." **Describe** the style of this celebration song.

We Wish You a Merry Christmas

Carol from England

1., 5. We wish you a mer-ry Christ-mas, We wish you a mer-ry Christ-mas,
2. Now bring us some fig-gy pud-ding, Now bring us some fig-gy pud-ding,

We wish you a mer-ry Christ-mas, And a hap-py New Year!
Now bring us some fig-gy pud-ding, And _ bring it out here.

REFRAIN

Good tid-ings we bring to you and your kin;

D.C. al Fine

We wish you a Mer-ry Christ-mas, And a hap-py New Year!

3. For we love our figgy pudding, *(3 times)*
   So bring some out here.
   Refrain

4. We won't go until we get some, *(3 times)*
   So bring some out here.
   Refrain

Form Finder

Look for the words *verse* and *refrain* in "We Wish You a Merry Christmas." How many times do you perform each section? **Move** to show the form of verse and refrain.

Christmas in Many Places

Here's a Jamaican Christmas song with words you might not know. *Lama* is the Jamaican word for presents. *Deggeday* is the word for dress-up clothes. Sing "Chrismus a Come."

CD 14–8

Chrismus a Come

Traditional Song from Jamaica

Chris - mus a come, me wan __ me la - ma,

Chris - mus a come, me wan __ me la - ma,

Chris - mus a come, me wan __ me deg - ge - day,

Chris - mus a come, me wan __ me deg - ge - day.

Christmas Beat

Now play this ostinato to accompany "Chrismus a Come." Tap and say the rhythm, then play it.

It's Almost Here!

Sometimes it's hard to wait for a special holiday. Sing along with "Almost Day," a song about waiting for Christmas. Then create your own ostinato to accompany the song.

CD 14–10

Almost Day

Words and Music by Huddie Ledbetter

1. Chick-ens crow-in' for mid-night, it's al-most day,
Refrain: Chick-ens crow-in' for mid-night, it's al-most day.

Chick-ens crow-in' for mid-night, it's al-most day. *(to Refrain)*
Chick-ens crow-in' for mid-night, it's al-most day. *(to Verse)*

2. Santa Claus is comin', it's almost day. . .
   Refrain

3. Think I heard my ma say it's almost day. . .
   Refrain

4. Think I heard my pa say it's almost day. . .
   Refrain

Holidays to Share

Posada, Piñata, Presents

Las posadas is part of the Christmas celebration in Mexico. Children carry small religious figures from house to house. Then they have a party with a *piñata* game. A *piñata* is a papier-mâché figure with candy and toys inside. **Sing** "*La piñata*." **Move** to show the tempo changes as you play the game.

Arts Connection

La piñata
by Diego Rivera
(1886–1957) ▼

CD 14–12

La piñata
(The *Piñata*)

English Words by Alice Firgau　　　　　　　　　　　　*Folk Song from Mexico*

VERSE

1. En las no-ches de po-sa-das, La pi-ña-ta es lo me-jor: _____
1. On *po-sa-da* nights we have such fun, The *pi-ña-ta* is the best of all.

Aun las ni-ñas re-mil-ga-das Se an-i-man con gran fer-vor.
E-ven shy girls join with ev-'ry-one As we try to make it fall.

REFRAIN

Da-le, da-le, da-le, no pier-das el ti-no.
There's the big *pi-ña-ta*, See if you can whack it,

Mi-de la dis-tan-cia que hay en el ca-mi-no.
Turn and swing, you'll hit it, Hit it hard, you'll crack it.

Que si no le das de un pa-lo te em-pi-no,
And if you don't break it, I'll raise you up there like it,

¡Por-que tie-nes au-ra de pu-ro pe-pi-no!
Like a big *pi-ña-ta*. So you bet-ter strike it!

2. Con tus ojitos vendados
   Y en las manos un bastón;
   ¡La olla rómpela a pedazos!
   ¡No le tengas compasión!
   Refrain

2. Put a blindfold over both your eyes,
   Take a stick in both your hands.
   Break the pot and let the pieces fly!
   Show no mercy, that's the plan!
   Refrain

Cymbals and Drums for Christmas

What instruments would you choose to play for a celebration? **Listen** to this song from Spain. Identify the names of instruments in the song. Then **sing** "*Zumba, zumba.*"

▲ tambourine

▲ gong

hand drum ▶

▲ finger cymbals

CD 14–16

Zumba, zumba

English Words by Margaret Marks

Folk Song from Spain

REFRAIN

Zum-ba, zum - ba - le al pan-de - ro   al pan-de - ro y al ra - bel
Zum-ba, zum - ba! Strike the cym-bal. Zum-ba, zum - ba! Strike the gong.

to - ca   to - ca   la zam-bom-ba   da - le   da - le al al - mi - rez
Zum-ba, zum - ba! Beat the tim-bal and the tam-bou-rine and drum!

Play with the ABA Form

Look at "*Zumba, zumba.*" How many times do you sing the refrain? The verse? Find the word *Fine* for a clue.

Read these rhythms. **Play** them during the refrain of "*Zumba, zumba.*"

Read these rhythms. **Play** them during the verse of "*Zumba, zumba.*"

Holiday Happenings

Puerto Rican children sing *"Aguinaldo"* as they travel from house to house during festival days after Christmas. **Listen** to *"Aguinaldo,"* then **sing** the song.

 CD 14–20

Aguinaldo

*English Words courtesy of
CP Language Institute, New York*

Carol from Puerto Rico

1. Á - bre-me   la   puer - ta   Á - bre-me   la   puer - ta
1. O-pen up   the   front   door,   O-pen up   the   front   door,

Que lo quie - ro en - trar;   He he-cho   mis   pas - te - les
Let me en - ter   in.   I   have made *pas - te - les*

Y no quier - en   que   dar. ____   He he-cho   mis   pas - te - les
For my friends with - in. _____   I   have made *pas - te - les*

Y no   quier - en   que   dar. _____
For   my   friends   with   -   in. _____

Play for the Holiday

Create ostinatos to add more layers of sound to *"Aguinaldo."* Use these instruments.

REFRAIN

A la sa - len - de - ra,   *A la sa - len - de - ra,*
Oh, what joy I'm feel - ing,   Oh, what joy I'm feel - ing,

A la sa - len - de - ra,   *de mi co - ra - zón.*
Oh, what joy I'm feel - ing   deep with-in my heart.

2. *Si no tiene nada*
   Si no tiene nada
   Nada nos dará;
   Pero lo que queremos
   cariño y bondad.
   Pero lo que queremos
   cariño y bondad.
   Refrain

2. If you've no possessions,
   If you've no possessions,
   Nothing can you share,
   But give love and kindness,
   Gifts beyond compare,
   But give love and kindness,
   Gifts beyond compare.
   Refrain

Kwanzaa!

During *Kwanzaa* [KWAHN-zah], some African American families gather to celebrate their African heritage. They greet each other by saying *"Habari Gani,"* Swahili for "What's the news?" or "What's happening?" Identify skips in the song. Then **sing** *"Habari Gani."*

CD 14–24
MIDI 36

Habari Gani

Words and Music by James McBride

VERSE

1. Win-ter ___ is here, so Kwan-zaa ___ is near, Cel-e-
2. Peace be ___ un-to you, good things come true When you

brat-ing joy and love as a hap-py fam-i-ly.
spread your joy and love in a hap-py fam-i-ly.

Join us in our greet-ing with sev-en days of hol-i-day,
Self-de-ter-mi-na-tion, ___ liv-ing as a na-tion, too.

Shar-ing all our gifts and love in a hap-py gath-er-ing.
We're all one re-la-tion and ___ live in har-mo-ny.

What's the Answer?

During *Kwanzaa,* there are special answers to the question *"Habari Gani?"* The answer is different for each of the seven days and nights of the celebration.

Umoja [oo-MOE-jah]	Unity
Kujichagulia [koo-jee-cha-goo-LEE-ah]	Self-determination
Ujima [oo-JEE-mah]	Collective work and responsibility
Ujamaa [oo-JAH-mah]	Sharing
Nia [nee-AH]	Purpose
Kuumba [koo-OOM-bah]	Creativity
Imani [ee-MAH-nee]	Faith

REFRAIN

Hap-py *Kwan-zaa!* Hap-py *Kwan-zaa!* Love and peace ___ from me to you. *Ha-ba-ri Ga-ni* spreads the news ___ of joy to you and asks "What's new?" new?"

3.

new?" "What's new?" *Ha-ba-ri Ga-ni!*

Element: TIMBRE | **Skill: LISTENING** | **Connection: CULTURE**

Happy New Year!

New Year's Day in Japan is a time for visiting friends and relatives. People wish each other good luck and send good luck cards. New Year's Day celebrations include music festivals. **Listen** for the timbre of Japanese instruments in *"Ichi-gatsu tsuitachi."*

CD 14–26
MIDI 37

Ichi-gatsu tsuitachi
(A New Year's Greeting)

Words by Senge Takatomi
English Words Adapted by Katherine S. Bolt

Music by Ue Sanemichi
School Song from Japan

と し の は じ め の た め し と て
To - shi no ha - ji - me no Ta - me - shi to - te
"O - me - de - to go - zai - mas," we will bow and say,

お わ り な き よ の め で た さ を
O - wa - ri na - ki yo no Me - de - ta - sa o
"O - me - de - to go - zai - mas," Hap - py New Year's Day.

Tune In

At midnight on New Year's Day, temple gongs in Japan are rung 108 times to chase away greed.

Listen to this song played on Japanese instruments. It is a duet for *koto* [KOH-toh] and *shakuhachi* [shah-koo-HAH-chee].

CD 14–30
Yamaji

by Kozo Masuda

This piece represents the composer's view of the Japanese countryside.

まつ　たけ　た　て　て　か　ど　ご　と　に
Mat - su - ta - ke ta - te te Ka - do go - to ni
Let us place our pine branch-es here be - side the door,

い　おぅ　きょう　こ　そ　た　の　し　け　れ
I - wo____ kyo____ ko - so Ta - no - shi - ke - re.
And wish our friends and neigh-bors man - y new years more.

Honoring a King

"Keep Your Eyes on the Prize" is a song from the civil rights movement of the 1960s. Think about what the prize is while you **sing** this song.

CD 14–31
MIDI 38

Keep Your Eyes on the Prize

African American Freedom Song

VERSE

Cm   Fm   Cm

1. Got my hand on the free - dom plow,
2. We fought jail and ___ vio - lence too,

Cm   Fm   Cm

Won't give no - thin' for my jour - ney now.
But God's love ___ has ___ seen us through.

Cm   G₇   Cm

Keep your eyes on ___ the prize. Hold on!
Keep your eyes on ___ the prize. Hold on!

An American Hero

Martin Luther King, Jr., fought for equal rights for African American people. He led non-violent protests and made speeches to inspire the civil rights movement.

Many songs have been written about Martin Luther King. **Listen** for the message of hope in *Shed a Little Light*.

CD 14–33
Shed a Little Light

by James Taylor

In this song, Martin Luther King's message is the "light" that helps us see how we can work together for freedom and equality.

▲ In 1964, Martin Luther King, Jr., received the Nobel Peace Prize for his leadership.

REFRAIN   Gm   Cm

Hold   on!   Hold   on!

            Cm   G7   Cm

Keep your eyes   on __ the prize. Hold   on!

3. Work all day and work all night,
   Tryin' to gain our civil rights.
   Keep your eyes on the prize.
   Hold on! *Refrain*

4. The only chain that a man can stand
   Is the chain of a hand in hand.
   Keep your eyes on the prize.
   Hold on! *Refrain*

Holdays to Share

Sing for Right

Before the civil rights movement, African Americans in some communities were not allowed to sit together with white people on buses. One day Rosa Parks, an African American woman, refused to move from the front of the bus to the back. Her example helped others have the courage to fight for their rights as American citizens.

Sing this song that honors Rosa Parks.

Back of the Bus

CD 15–1

Traditional Song
Adapted by Miss Mary Jane Pigee

1. If you miss ___ me on the back of the bus, ___
2. If you miss ___ me on the back of the bus, ___

and you can find _____ me no - where,
and you can find _____ me no - where,

Come on up ___ to the front of the bus, ___ I'll be rid - in' up there.
Come on up ___ to the driv - er's seat, ___ I'll be driv - ing there.

I'll be rid - in' up there, I'll be rid - in' up there.
I'll be driv - ing there, I'll be driv - ing there.

Come on up __ to the front of the bus, __ I'll be rid - in' up there.
Come on up __ to the driv - er's seat, __ I'll be driv - ing there.

A Musical Tribute

Listen to *Sister Rosa*. How do the performers use *staccato* and *legato* sounds to create a sense of pride?

CD 15–3

Sister Rosa

by the Neville Brothers

The Neville Brothers use rap style in this tribute to Rosa Parks.

Holidays to Share

Sing of Liberty!

What does *liberty* mean? Look for clues as you **sing** this patriotic song.

CD 15–4

America

Words by Samuel Francis Smith

Traditional Melody

1. My coun - try! 'tis of thee, Sweet land of lib - er - ty,
2. My na - tive coun - try, thee, Land of the no - ble free,
3. Let mu - sic swell the breeze, And ring from all the trees

Of thee I sing; Land where my fa - thers died,
Thy name I love; I love thy rocks and rills,
Sweet Free - dom's song; Let mor - tal tongues a - wake,

Land of the Pil - grims' pride, From ev - 'ry ____
Thy woods and tem - pled hills; My heart __ with __
Let all that breathe par - take. Let rocks __ their __

moun - tain - side Let ____ free - dom ring!
rap - ture thrills Like ____ that a - bove.
si - lence break, The ____ sound pro - long.

America, the Beautiful is a song celebrating the beauty of our country. How would you describe the tempo of this song?

CD 15–6

America, the Beautiful

Words by Katharine Lee Bates

Music by Samuel A. Ward

1. O beau-ti-ful for spa-cious skies, For am-ber waves of grain,
2. O beau-ti-ful for pa-triot dream That sees be-yond the years

For pur-ple moun-tain maj-es-ties A-bove the fruit-ed plain!
Thine al-a-bas-ter cit-ies gleam, Un-dimmed by hu-man tears!

A-mer-i-ca! A-mer-i-ca! God shed His grace on thee,

And crown thy good with broth-er-hood From sea to shin-ing sea!

Listen to this version of *America, the Beautiful.* How is it different from the first version you heard?

CD 15–8

America, the Beautiful

by Katherine Lee Bates and Samuel A. Ward

This version of *America the Beautiful* is sung in gospel style.

Yankee Doodle Days

Patriotic songs celebrate our country. **Move** to show the meter of "Yankee Doodle." Then **sing** it for fun!

CD 15–9

Yankee Doodle

Words by Dr. Richard Shuckburgh   *Traditional*

VERSE

1. ᵧ Fath'r and I went down to camp, A - long with Cap - tain Good-in',
2. And there we saw a thou-sand men, As rich as Squire __ Da - vid;

And there we saw the men and boys As thick as hast - y pud - din'.
And what they wast-ed ev - 'ry day, I wish it could be sav - ed.

REFRAIN

Yan - kee Doo - dle, keep it up, Yan - kee Doo - dle dan - dy,

Mind the mu - sic and the step And with the girls be hand - y.

3. And there was Captain Washington
    Upon a slapping stallion,
    A-giving orders to his men;
    I guess there was a million. *Refrain*

Sing About Our Flag

Sing "The Star-Spangled Banner," our national anthem.

 CD 15–12 The Star-Spangled Banner

Words by Francis Scott Key

Music by John Stafford Smith

Music Reading Practice

Reading Sequence 1, page 12

CD 1–12
MIDI 39

Rhythm: Reading ♩, ♫ ♩, and 𝄽

Use rhythm syllables to **read** and **perform** these rhythms with "Alligator Pie."

Reading Sequence 2, page 14

CD 1–17
MIDI 40

Rhythm: Reading ♩♬

Read and **perform** this exercise using rhythm syllables. Then **play** the rhythms on percussion instruments as you sing "Ding, Dong, Diggidiggidong."

CD 1–45
MIDI 41

Melody: Reading *mi*, *re*, and *do*

Use pitch syllables to **read** and **sing** this melody with the refrain of "Oh, Won't You Sit Down."

CD 1–50
MIDI 42

Reading Sequence 4, page 30

Melody: Reading *do*-Pentatonic

Read and **sing** this simple version of "Ida Red" to practice inner hearing.

Reading Sequence 5, page 52

CD 2–23
MIDI 43

Rhythm: Reading

Read and **perform** this exercise with "Black Snake."

Reading Sequence 6, page 54

CD 2–28
MIDI 44

Rhythm: Reading

Read and **perform** this exercise with "Mister Ram Goat-O" using rhythm syllables.

CD 2–45
MIDI 45

Melody: Reading *low la*

Use pitch syllables and hand signs to **read** and **sing** this exercise with "One Morning Soon."

CD 2–51
MIDI 46

Melody: Reading *low la*

Read and **sing** this melody with "*Hosisipa*" using pitch syllables and hand signs.

CD 3–27
MIDI 47

Reading Sequence 9, page 92

Rhythm: Reading

Use rhythm syllables to **read** and **perform** these rhythms with "Chicken on the Fence Post."

CD 3–33
MIDI 48

Reading Sequence 10, page 94

Rhythm: Reading   and

Read and **perform** this exercise using rhythm syllables.
Then **play** the rhythms on percussion instruments as you sing "Love Somebody."

CD 4–5

MIDI 49

Melody: Reading *low so*

Read and **sing** this exercise with *"Hwa yuan li-de young wa wa"*
to practice inner hearing.

CD 4–11

MIDI 50

Melody: Reading *low so*

Use pitch syllables and hand signs to **read** and **sing** this
countermelody for "Alabama Gal."

421

Music Reading Practice

Reading Sequence 13, page 128

CD 4–37
MIDI 51

Rhythm: Reading ♩, ♫, and ♩. in ¾

Read and **perform** these rhythms with "Morning Is Come."

Reading Sequence 14, page 130

CD 4–42
MIDI 52

Rhythm: Reading Rhythms in ¾

Conduct a three-beat pattern as you sing "The Juniper Tree."
Then **read** and **perform** this exercise using rhythm syllables.

Melody: Reading *high do*

Use pitch syllables and hand signs to **read** and **sing** this countermelody for "Li'l Liza Jane."

Melody: Reading *do* and *high do*

Read and **sing** this countermelody for "Hop Up, My Ladies" to practice inner hearing.

CD 6–5
MIDI 55

Reading Sequence 17, page 166

Rhythm: Reading Rhythms in $\frac{2}{4}$

Use rhythm syllables to **read** and **perform** these rhythms with
"Don't Let Your Watch Run Down."

Fine

D.C. al Fine

CD 6–10
MIDI 56

Reading Sequence 18, page 168

Rhythm: Reading Rhythms in $\frac{3}{4}$ and $\frac{2}{4}$

Read and **perform** this exercise using rhythm syllables.
Then **play** the rhythms on percussion instruments as you sing
"Coffee Grows on White Oak Trees."

Fine

D.C. al Fine

Reading Sequence 19, page 180

CD 6–24
MIDI 57

Melody: Reading a *do*-Pentatonic Song

Read and **sing** this melody with "Don't Let the Wind" using pitch syllables and hand signs.

Reading Sequence 20, page 182

CD 6–31
MIDI 58

Melody: Reading a *la*-Pentatonic Song

Use pitch syllables and hand signs to **read** and **sing** this countermelody for *"Erdö, erdö de magos."*

| la | so | mi | re | do | la, |

| la, | do | do | re | mi | re | do | do | mi |

| la, | do | do | re | mi | re | do | do | re |

| la | so | mi | re | do | la, |

Music Reading Practice

Reading Sequence 21, page 204

CD 7–14
MIDI 59

Rhythm: Reading Rhythms in $\frac{4}{4}$

Read and **perform** these rhythms with "Turn the Glasses Over."

Reading Sequence 22, page 206

CD 7–21
MIDI 60

Rhythm: Reading Upbeats

Read and **perform** this exercise with *"Hashkediya"* using rhythm syllables. Does it begin on an upbeat or a downbeat?

CD 7–35

MIDI 61

Melody: Reading a *so*-Pentatonic Song

Read and **sing** this exercise with "Pretty Saro" to practice inner hearing using pitch syllables and hand signs.

| so, | la, | do | do | la, | so, | do | re | mi | so |

| so, | la, | do | do | la, | do | re | re | mi | re |

| mi | mi | mi | re | do | la, | do | la, | do | re |

| so, | la, | do | do | la, | so, | do | do | la, | so, |

CD 7–40

MIDI 62

Melody: Reading Letter Names B-A-G

Use pitch syllables and hand signs to **read** and **sing** this melody with "Hot Cross Buns (Version 1)." Then sing it with letter names.

Playing the Recorder

Getting Ready

This section of your book will help you learn to **play** the soprano recorder, a small wind instrument.

To get started, try this trick!
- Extend your hand forward with palm upward.
- Pretend you have a small feather on your palm.
- Blow the feather gently so it moves across your palm without falling.

This is all the air you need to produce a good sound.

Covering the Holes

Using your left hand, cover the holes shown in the picture. Be sure to press just hard enough so that the holes make a light mark on your fingers. Remove your hand to check that there is an outline of a circle on each finger. Hold the bottom of the recorder with your right hand, balancing it with your thumb and pinky. Don't cover the bottom holes.

G

Let's Play G

Put your hands in position to play G. Cover the tip of the mouthpiece with your lips. Blow gently as you whisper *daah*. Practice playing G using a steady beat pattern of quarter notes.

Play this pattern throughout the verse of "Li'l Liza Jane" (page 140).

G

Patterns on G

Play this ostinato throughout "*Kum bachur atzel*" (page 138). Whisper *daah* on each note so you can hear a short–short–long pattern.

G

Adding A

Look at the diagrams for G and A. **Play** G for four beats, followed by four beats of A. When you uncover the third hole, what happens to the sound of your recorder?

G   A

Playing A and G

You are now ready to **play** a **countermelody** during the verses of "Old Dan Tucker" (page 96).

> A **countermelody** is a different melody that is played or sung at the same time as the main melody.

Ready for B

Now you are ready to learn to **play** B. Cover the holes shown in the diagram. Will B sound higher or lower than G and A?

B

Here is a recorder part that you can play while others sing "*Ahora voy a cantarles*" (page 56).

"B-A-G" Songs

Now that you can play B, A, and G, you will be able to **play** "Hot Cross Buns" (page 218).

Building Right Hand Strength

Here are two new notes. Be sure to have your left hand on the top and the right hand below. Cover the holes securely with your fingers slightly arched as you whisper *daah*.

D

E

Now you are ready to **play** a countermelody to accompany the refrain of "Joy to the World" (page 23).

D　　　　　　**E**

Recorder Long Ago

The lute and recorder were instruments heard in the royal courts of Europe beginning in the late 1400s and early 1500s.

Listen to *Sonata Seconda*. Is the recorder playing mostly long or mostly short sounds?

CD 15–14
Sonata Seconda

by Dario Castello

This piece is played on soprano recorder and lute. It was written in the 1600s.

431

Mallet Instruments

Many Mallets to Choose

Mallets are percussion sticks with different types of heads. Some heads are wrapped with yarn, some are hard wood, plastic, hard rubber, or metal. The type of mallet you use to play an instrument will affect its timbre.

Since glockenspiels have a high, bright sound, you can use wooden-headed mallets to produce a warm, clear sound.

▲ Alto glockenspiel
with wooden mallets

Sound Choices

Xylophones and metallophones can be played with either soft-headed or hard-headed mallets, depending on the type of sound you want to produce. What kind of sound do you think a hard-headed mallet will make?

▼ Alto metallophone

▲ Soprano xylophone

Be careful to choose mallets that are the right size for the instrument. If the bars bounce when you strike them, the mallets are probably too large.

Bass xylophone ▶

Time to Play!

Play this **bordun** on the alto xylophone. What kind of mallet will you choose?

L   R   L   R

A **bordun** is a repeated pattern used to accompany music. It has two pitches, one of which is the home tone.

Be sure to hold the mallets with a relaxed grip.

Sound Bank

Caja [KAH-hah] A short, squat drum made from a hollow log, with two drumheads. The player uses two sticks to strike one head and the side of the drum. The drum is often placed on the ground and held with one foot while the performer plays. CD 15–15

Cello [CHEHL-oh] A large wooden string instrument. The cello may be plucked with fingers or played with a bow. The cello has a rich, warm sound and can play quite low. CD 15–16

Clarinet An instrument shaped like a long cylinder. It is usually made of wood with a reed in the mouthpiece. The clarinet's low notes are soft and hollow. The highest notes are thin and piercing. CD 15–17

Conga [KAHN-gah] An Afro-Cuban drum with a long barrel-shaped body. It comes in two sizes: the small *quinto* and the large *tumbador*. The conga is struck with the fingers and the palms of the hands. CD 15–18

Instrument Key: strings percussion woodwind brass

Flute A small, metal instrument shaped like a pipe. The player holds the flute sideways and blows across an open mouthpiece. The flute's voice is clear and sweet. CD 15–19

Flute (Native American) An end-blown instrument made from a wooden tube. Part of the upper end of the tube is cut out to make the sound. Finger holes along the body help the player change pitches. This flute sounds very much like a recorder. CD 15–20

French Horn A medium-sized instrument made of coiled brass tubing. At one end is a large bell; at the other end is a mouthpiece. The sound of the horn is mellow and warm. CD 15–21

Guitar A wooden instrument with six nylon or steel strings. The player strums or plucks the strings with a pick or the fingers. You can use a guitar to play a melody. You can also play chords to accompany a melody. CD 15–22

Guitarrón [gee-tah-ROHN] A large bass guitar with a round back. It is strung with six harp strings and is played in Mexican *mariachi* groups. CD 15–23

Harpsichord A keyboard instrument shaped like a piano. When the keys are pressed, the strings inside the instrument are plucked by small quills. This gives the sound a tinkling quality. CD 15–24

Irish Harp A small, triangular-shaped stringed instrument. The strings are made of brass or gut. They are strummed or plucked. CD 15–25

Jarana [ha-RAH-nah] An eight-string guitar used in folk music of Mexico. It is strummed or plucked with the fingers. CD 15–26

Koto [KOH-toh] A Japanese string instrument with seven to seventeen long strings. These are set high above the body of the instrument, which sits flat on the floor. The sound is a little like that of a harp. CD 15–27

Marimba A large, barred instrument played with mallets. The bars are made of rosewood, with long resonating tubes that hang below each bar. The marimba has a mellow ringing sound. CD 15–28

Panpipes A wind instrument that consists of a set of hollow tubes of different lengths tied together. Sound is produced by blowing across the open upper ends. Each tube has its own pitch. The longer the tube, the lower its pitch. CD 15–29

Instrument Key: strings   percussion   woodwind   brass

Piano A large keyboard instrument with strings inside. When the keys are pressed, hammers in the piano hit the strings to make them sound. CD 15–30

Pujador [POO-hah-dohr] A medium-sized drum from Panama. It has one drumhead, and is held between the knees and hit with the hands. CD 15–31

Repicador [reh-PEEK-ah-dohr] A small drum from Panama. It is tapered, with one drumhead. It is held between the knees and hit with the hands. CD 15–32

Requinto [reh-KEEN-toh] A small guitar similar to a ukulele. It has four strings that are plucked with a long, thin pick. The requinto often plays very fast melodies. CD 15–33

Shakuhachi [shah-koo-HAH-chee] A Japanese flute made of bamboo. The *shakuhachi* is played with lots of pitch bends, clicks, and flutters. It sounds like a human singing voice and can produce unusual, airy sounds. CD 15–34

Sound Bank

◀ **Snare Drum** A small, cylinder-shaped drum with two heads. Snares (strings wrapped with wire) are stretched across the bottom head to create a vibrating sound. A snare drum can make a long, raspy roll or a sharp, rhythmic beating sound. CD 15–35

◀ **String Bass** A large, wooden string instrument that is either plucked or bowed. The string bass is so tall that the player must stand up or sit on a high stool to play it. The voice of the string bass is deep, dark, and sometimes rumbling. CD 15–36

◀ **Timpani** Large, pot-shaped drums, also called kettle-drums. Unlike most drums, timpani can be tuned to notes of the scale. The timpani's voice can sound like a loud boom, a quiet thump, or a distant rumble. CD 15–37

◀ **Trombone** A brass instrument with a large bell at one end of the tubing and a long, curved slide. The trombone can be loud and brilliant, but its soft voice is mellow. CD 15–38

◀ **Trumpet** A brass instrument with a bell at one end of its coiled tubing. The trumpet's voice can be loud and bright, but can also sound warm and sweet. CD 15–39

Instrument Key: strings   percussion   woodwind   brass

◀ **Tuba** A large brass instrument with a wide bell at one end of coiled tubing. The tuba's low notes are soft and dark-sounding. The higher ones are full and warm.
CD 15–40

◀ **Vibraphone** A keyboard of metal bars played with mallets. Resonating tubes hang below each bar. A metal fan moves air through the tubes to create a vibrating sound. CD 15–41

◀ **Viola** [vee-OH-luh] A wooden string instrument that looks like a large violin. The viola is either bowed or plucked. The sound of the viola is deeper, richer, and darker than that of the violin. CD 15–42

◀ **Violin** A small, wooden string instrument that is held under the player's chin. The violin plays sounds from low to very high. A good player can create many unusual and interesting sounds on the violin. CD 15–43

◀ **Xylophone** A keyboard of wooden bars played with mallets. The xylophone has a bright, brittle sound.
CD 15–44

Sound Bank

Glossary

Highlighted terms appear as vocabulary words on the indicated lesson pages.

AB form A musical plan that has two different parts, or sections. p. 20

ABA form A musical plan that has three sections. The first and last sections are the same. The middle section is different. p. 134

accent An accent is used to give emphasis to a single note. p. 209

accompaniment A part, usually played by one or more instruments, that supports a main melody. p. 36

arco Playing a string instrument with the bow. p. 113

ballad A song that tells a story. p. 352

bar lines ≡ The up and down lines in a piece of music that show how beats are grouped together. p. 131

beat The regular pulse felt in most music. p. 10

bordun A repeated pattern used to accompany music. It has two pitches, one of which is the home tone. p. 433

call and response A form of choral singing. The call is sung by a leader. The response is usually sung by a group. p. 58

canon A follow-the-leader process in which all perform the same pattern, but start at different times. p. 190

chord A group of three or more pitches sounding at the same time. p. 227

coda Music that ends a song after the words are sung. p. 138

countermelody A different melody that is played or sung at the same time as the main melody. p. 430

crescendo ◁ A sign that tells you to get louder. p. 200

D.C. al Fine An Italian musical term that tells you to go back to the beginning of the song and repeat until the word *Fine*. p. 101

decrescendo ▷ A sign that tells you to get softer. p. 200

double bar The up and down double lines that mark the end of a song. p. 131

downbeat The beat that begins a measure. p. 207

dynamics The louds and softs in music. p. 6

form The overall plan of a piece of music. p. 20

harmony Two or more different pitches sounding at the same time. p. 225

improvise To make up music as it is being performed. p. 119

introduction Music that is played before the words are sung. p. 138

legato Smooth and connected sounds. p. 87

measure ▭ The space between two bar lines. p. 131

melodic ostinato A melody pattern that repeats several times. p. 115

melody A line of single tones that move up, down, or repeat. p. 24

meter The way beats of music are grouped, often in sets of two or three. p. 169

octave The distance between one note and the next higher or lower note that has the same name. p. 143

ostinato A repeated rhythm or melody pattern. p. 41

partner songs Two or more different songs that can be sung at the same time to create harmony. p. 152

pentatonic Songs that have only five pitches. p. 30

phrase A musical sentence. p. 18

pizzicato Plucking the strings of an instrument with the fingers. p. 113

refrain A song part that is sung the same way every time it repeats. p. 97

repeated pitches Two or more pitches in a row that are the same. p. 65

rests Symbols for silences in music. p. 12

rhythm A pattern of long and short sounds and silences. p. 10

rondo A musical form in which the A section repeats between two or more contrasting sections. p. 210

scat A style of jazz singing where nonsense syllables take the place of words. p. 158

skip Moving from one pitch to another, skipping the pitches in between. p. 64

staccato Short and separated sounds. p. 87

step A move from one pitch to another without skipping a pitch. p. 64

strong beat The first beat in a measure. p. 128

style The special sound that is created when musical elements such as rhythm, timbre, and expression are combined. p. 44

subito A sudden change. p. 125

syncopation Rhythm where the note that is stressed comes between two beats. p. 55

tempo The speed of the beat. p. 50

texture How thin or thick music sounds. It is created by layering sounds on top of each other. p. 79

tie A musical symbol that joins two notes together to create a longer sound. p. 53

timbre The special sound each voice or instrument makes. p. 73

tonal center The home tone of a song. p. 215

unison When all instruments or voices play or sing the same notes. p. 113

upbeat One or more notes before the first strong beat of a phrase. p. 133

verse A song part where the melody stays the same when it repeats, but the lyrics change. p. 97

Classified Index

Listening selections appear in *italics*.

Poems and Stories

Recorded Interviews

Credits

Design and Electronic Production: Kirchoff/Wohlberg, Inc.

Listening Maps and Music Reading Practice: MediaLynx Design Group

Photograph Credits

4 M. & E. Bernheim/Woodfin Camp & Associates 4 © Tony Freeman/PhotoEdit 4 PhotoDisc 5 Daemmrich Photography 5 © Lindsay Hebberd/Woodfin Camp & Associates 5 Paul Thompson/ImageState 6 Everett Collection, Inc. 8 Everett Collection, Inc. 9 Everett Collection, Inc. 12 (TR) © Dave G. Houser/Houserstock, Inc. 17 (B) ©Dorling Kindersley 25 © Archivo Iconografico, S.A./Corbis 33 Liaison Agency 33 Liaison Agency 36 Getty Images 37 Getty Images 38 Osamu Honda/AP/Wide World 39 Brian Hennessey/Sony Classical 44 (C) Corbis 44 (TL) Corbis 45 (BR) Getty Images 46 (Bkgd) Corbis 46 (TL) Liz McAulay/©Dorling Kindersley 53 © Joe Viesti/Viesti Collection, Inc. 56 © Joe Viesti/Viesti Collection, Inc. 57 © Joe Viesti/Viesti Collection, Inc. 67 © Neal Preston/Corbis 70 Werner Forman Archive/The Bradford Coll., Plains Indian Museum, BBHC, Cody, Wyoming, USA/Art Resource, NY 70 ©Richard A. Cooke/Corbis 72 Getty Images 72 Ian Shaw/Stone 73 Getty Images 73 Ian Shaw/Stone 74 R. Brandon/Alaska Stock 74 Getty Images 74 © Dorling Kindersley 75 Nancy Brown/Singer/Songwriter Tom Chapin 75 © Dorling Kindersley 76 (Bkgd) Richard Hamilton Smith/Corbis82 Metronome/Archive Photos 82 © Dan Scafidi/Drum Corps International 82 ©Bettmann/Corbis 82 Frances Kaplan Moore 82 © D. Roundtree/Image Bank 82 Getty Images 89 Scala/Art Resource, NY 89 Christie's, London/SuperStock 89 William Johnson/Stock Boston 105 Li Mei-Shu Foundation 109 (B) ©Elizabeth Zuckerman/PhotoEdit 114 Getty Images 117 Photofest 132 SuperStock 136 ©Jack Vartoogian 137 Victoria & Albert Museum, London/Art Resource, NY145 Bettmann/Corbis149 ©Gavin Smith/FSP/Gamma/Liaison Agency 150 ©Jack Vartoogian 150 Getty Images 151 ©Bertrano LaForet/Liaison Agency 156 Getty Images 161 (BR) Frank Driggs Collection 166 Corbis 167 Hulton-Deutsch Collection/Corbis 167 Corbis 177 Frederic Remington Art Museum, Ogdensburg, New York 184 Japanese Music Institute of America 184 A.S.K./Viesti Collection, Inc. 185 Jack Vartoogian 185 David Young-Wolff/PhotoEdit 186 Getty Images 188 Summit Records 189 Cylla von Tiedemann/ICM Artists, Ltd. 196 (BR) Mary Kate Denny/PhotoEdit 196 (TR) Paul S. Conklin/Paul S. Conklin 197 (BC) Corbis 197 (TL) ©Kevin Schafer/Corbis 198 (TR) ©Annie Griffiths Belt/Corbis 200 © Jim Bush/Buffalo Philharmonic Orchestra 209 Jack Vartoogian 209 Gerard Del Vecchio/Stone 236 Teri Bloom Photography, Inc 236 @2000 John Running 236 Bob Daemmrich/Daemmrich Photography 236 © Torleif Svensson/The Stock Market 237 © Ken Biggs/Stone 241 Globe Photos, Inc. 241 Drew/AP/Wide World 247 Indianapolis Children's Choir 249 Robert Brenner/PhotoEdit 249 Bettmann/Corbis 250 (Bkgd) ©Steve Bein/Corbis 250 (TR) Geoff Brightling/©Dorling Kindersley 251 (CR) Geoff Brightling/©Dorling Kindersley 251 (BR) Gjon Mili/Time Life Pictures/Getty Images 252 (TL) ©Myron Jay Dorf/Corbis 255 @2000 John Running 257 Corbis 269 © Dorling Kindersley 273 Michael S. Yamashita/Corbis 273 Paul A. Souders/Corbis 274 ©Jack Vartoogian 275 (TCR) Cyril Laubscher/©Dorling Kindersley 281 © Migdoll 281 © Bettmann/Corbis 283 Ulrike Welsch 283 Robert Fried Photography 283 ©Victor Englebert 288 The Newark Museum, Newark, New Jersey, USA/Art Resource 289 Crispin Hughes/Hutchison Library 289 ©Lawrence Migdale/Stone 289 Pictorial Press 292 Courtesy of Vanguard Records, a/Welk Music Group Company 295 Getty Images 296 (Bkgd) ©Michael Busselle/Corbis 301 © Rick Poley/Visuals Unlimited 304 SuperStock 309 Courtesy Joao Baptista Felga de Moraes 317 (C) ©Paul Almasy/Corbis 318 Owen Franken/Corbis 319 Monica Maynard 324 © Gary Bartholomew/Corbis 324 TSS/NASA/The Stock Solution 326 ARC Science/The Stock Solution 332 (Bkgd) ©Ric Ergenbright/Corbis 350 Spencer Grant/PhotoEdit 350 SuperStock 351 © Myrleen Ferguson Cate/PhotoEdit 351 © David Young-Wolff/PhotoEdit 351 © Bonnie Kamin 356 ©Erich Lessing/Art Resource, NY 357 The Granger Collection, New York 362 (Bkgd) William J. Hebert/Getty Images 364 Illustration from ZOMO THE RABBIT, copyright © 1992 by Gerald McDermott, reprinted by permission of Harcourt, Inc. 370 ©David Atlas 379 © Fabian Falcon/Stock Boston 379 Jeff Day 382 Tom & DeeAnn McCarthy/The Stock Market 383 Ariel Skelley/The Stock Market 383 SuperStock 398 (BC) Schalkwijk/Art Resource, NY 400 (CL) Andy Crawford©Horniman Museum and Garden/©Dorling Kindersley 400 (TL) Philip Dowell/©Dorling Kindersley 400 (TC) Corbis 403 (TR) Jeremy Horner/Corbis 404 Getty Images 406 Milt & Joan Mann/Cameramann International, Ltd. 406 Keyphotos/The Stock Market 406 Milt & Joan Mann/Cameramann International, Ltd. 407 Milt & Joan Mann/Cameramann International, Ltd. 407 Keyphotos/The Stock Market 408 Corbis 408 AP/Wide World 409 AP/Wide World 410 UPI/Corbis 410 © Bettmann/Corbis 411 ©Bettmann/Corbis 412 © Ron Watts/Corbis 431 Robert von Bahr/Robert Von Bahr/BIS Records AB

Credits/Illustrations

2 Elizabeth Sayles 6 Rusty Fletcher 8 Rusty Fletcher 10 Tom Barrett 12 Judy Jarrett 13 Bernard Adnet 14 Karen Stormer Brooks 15 Karen Stormer Brooks 16 Ruth Nagle 19 Ruth Nagle 20 Annette Cable 22 Annette Cable 24 Steven Mach 26 Steven Mach 27 Joe Rogers 28 Lauren Uram 30 Georgia Cawley 31 Joe Rogers 32 Ilene Richard 33 Ilene Richard 34 Ilene Richard 35 Ilene Richard 40 Leon Zernitsky 42 Ruth Nagle 43 Steven Mach 48 Kathleen O'Malley 50 Kathleen O'Malley 51 Kathleen O'Malley 52 Will Terry 54 Francesco Santalucia 55 Ruth Nagle 56 Lindy Burnett 59 Ruth Nagle 60 Lindy Burnett 64 Stephanie Power 68 Stacey Schuett 70 Ruth Nagle 71 Ruth Nagle 72 Russell Charpentier 73 Russell Charpentier 75 Russell Charpentier 78 Dennis Hockerman 80 Kathleen O'Malley 86 Tiphanie Beeke 88 Gershom Griffith 92 Jared Lee 96 Scott Peck 96 Georgia

Cawley 98 Christopher Corr 98 Scott Peck 102 Anthony Carnabuci 104 Anthony Carnabuci 106 Richard Stergulz 108 Tom Leonard 110 Shelly Bartek 111 Anthony Carnabuci 116 Jody Wheeler 118 Tiphanie Beeke 119 Scott Peck 119 Tiphanie Beeke 120 Jerry Tiritilli 122 Jerry Tiritilli 124 Elizabeth Wolf 126 Wayne Parmenter 128 Susan Gaber 130 David Cunningham 134 Ruth Nagle 138 Lori Lohstoeter 140 Susan Greenstein 142 Scott Peck 144 Scott Peck 146 Higgins Bond 148 Tony Nuccio 149 Tony Nuccio 150 Tony Nuccio 151 Tony Nuccio 152 Anthony Lewis 153 Anthony Lewis 156 Scott Peck 158 William Ersland 160 William Ersland 167 Tony Nuccio 168 Carolyn Croll 169 Carolyn Croll 169 Christopher Kean 170 Annie Lunsford 170 Kelly Hume 171 Annie Lunsford 172 Annie Lunsford 173 Annie Lunsford 174 Brad Teare 174 Kelly Hume 176 Brad Teare 178 Jennifer Hewitson 180 Susan Swan 180 Kelly Hume 182 Susan Tolonen 190 Lydia Taranovic 191 Lydia Taranovic 192 Nancy Freeman 195 Lydia Taranovic 201 Guy Porfirio 202 Guy Porfirio 203 Guy Porfirio 205 Stephen Snider 220 Karen Pellaton 221 Karen Pellaton 224 Jill Meyerhoff 230 Roberta Arenson 232 Guy Porfirio 240 Franklin Hammond 247 Jon Conrad 249 Jon Conrad 258 Melinda Levine 262 Marnie Webster 271 Dan Durkin 284 Susan Tolonen 292 Eileen Mueller Neill 293 Gregg Thorkelson 298 Ilene Robinette 303 Sally Jo Vitsky 304 Tony Caldwell 312 Guy Porfirio 314 Susan Spellman 316 Susan Spellman 317 Susan Spellman 322 Betsy Day 328 Marjorie Muns 334 Douglas Klauba 338 Darryl Ligasan 340 Steven Mach 345 Naomi Howland 346 Naomi Howland 348 Joel Spector 350 Joel Spector 352 Gloria Calderon 354 John Sandford 354 Kelly Hume 355 John Sandford 356 John Sandford 358 Eileen Hine 360 Eileen Hine 364 Kelly Hume 366 Joseph Hammond 368 Rob Dunlavey 368 Kelly Hume 369 Rob Dunlavey 370 Rob Dunlavey 371 Rob Dunlavey 374 Franklin Hammond 376 Franklin Hammond 380 Marion Eldridge 382 Marion Eldridge 383 Marion Eldridge 384 Nora Koerber 386 Judith Mitchell 392 Donna Perrone 394 Donna Perrone 396 Fred Willingham 398 Melinda Levine 402 George Crespo 404 Paula Wendland 405 Paula Wendland 414 Ed Parker 415 Ed Parker

Acknowledgments

Credits and appreciation are due publishers and copyright owners for use of the following:

2: "Hello to the World" © 2002 Pearson Education, Inc. 4: "Hello to All the Children of the World", from We Sing Around the World by Pamela Conn Beall and Susan Hagen Nipp, copyright © 1994 by Pamela Conn Beall and Susan Hagen Nipp. Used by permission of Price Stern & Sloan, Inc., a division of Penguin Putnam Inc. 7: "Supercalifragilisticexpialidocious" Words and music by Richard M. Sherman and Robert B. Sherman. © 1963 Wonderland Music Company, Inc. All Rights Reserved. Reprinted by Permission. 10: "Name, Name, What's Your Name?" by Jim Solomon. Reprinted by Permission. 12: "Gypsy in the Moonlight" (Folk Song from Trinidad), from Caribbean Voyage: Brown Girl In The Ring. Courtesy of the Alan Lomax Archives. 13: "Alligator Pie" from Dinosaur Dinner (With A Slice Of Alligatator Pie) by Dennis Lee, copyright Compilation © 1997 by Alfred A. Knopf, Inc. Text © 1974, 1977, 1983, 1991 by Dennis Lee. Illustrations © 1997 by Debbie Tilley. Used by permission of Alfred A. Knopf, an imprint of Random House Children's Books, a division of Random House, Inc. Rhythmic setting © 2002 Pearson Education, Inc. 14: "Ding, Dong, Diggidiggidong" from Music for Children, Vol. 1, by Carl Orff and Gunild Keetman, English version adapted by Margaret Murray. Copyright © 1958 by Schott & Co., Ltd., London. Copyright renewed. All Rights Reserved. Used by permission of European American Distributors LLC, sole U.S. and Canadian agent for Schott & Co. Ltd., London. 15: "Cats" (excerpt) by Eleanor Farjeon. Reprinted by permission of Harold Ober Associates Incorporated. Copyright © 1957 by Eleanor Farjeon. 16: "Golden Ring Around Susan Girl" folk song sung by Jean Ritchie, from Folk Songs of the Southern Appalachians. © 1963 Jean Ritchie Geordie Music Publishing Company. Used by Permission. 20: "Ambos a dos" (Go Two by Two) English words © 1995 Silver Burdett Ginn. 22: "Joy To The World", Words and Music by Hoyt Axton. Copyright © 1970 by IRVING MUSIC, INC. Copyright Renewed. This arrangement Copyright © 2003 IRVING MUSIC, INC. All Rights Reserved. Used by Permission. 30: "Ida Red" from 150 American Folk Songs to Sing Read and Play. © Copyright 1974 by Boosey & Hawkes, Inc. Reprinted by permission of Boosey & Hawkes, Inc. 32: "Mud" from the poem, "Beavers in November" by Marilyn Singer from Turtle in July, (Simon & Schuster, 1989). Music © 2000 David Eddleman. All Rights Reserved. Reprinted by Permission. 33: "The Hippopotamus Song" by Michael Flanders and Donald Swann. © 1952 (Renewed) Chappell & Co. All rights administered by Chappell & Co. All Rights Reserved. Used by Permission. WARNER BROS. PUBLICATIONS U.S. INC., Miami, FL 33014. 35: "Grasshoppers" from Joyful Noise by Paul Fleischman. Text copyright © 1998 by Oaul Fleischman. Used by permission of Harper Collins Publishers. 40: "La pulga de San José" © 1994 José-Luis Orozco, Spanish lyrics and English lyrics and musical arrangement. All Rights Reserved. Used by Permission. Recordings for this selection and others by José-luis Orozco are available from Arcoris Records, P.O. Box 7482, Berkeley CA 94707. 43: "Rain" from Whispers and Other Poems by Myra Cohn Livingston. Copyright © 1958, 1986 Myra Cohn Livingston. Used by permission of Marian Reiner. 46: "Peppermint Twist" Words and Music by Joey Dee and Henry Glover. © 1961, 1962 (Copyrights Renewed) EMI Longitude Music Co. All Rights Reserved. Used by Permission. WARNER BROS. PUBLICATIONS U.S. INC., Miami, FL 33014. 54: "Mister Ram Goat-O" from Brown Girl in The Ring by Alan Lomax, J.D. Elder and Bess Lomax Hawes. Copyright © 1997 by Alan Lomax. Reprinted by permission of Pantheon Books, a division of Random House, Inc. 56: "Ahora voy a cantarles" (Now Hear the Song I'll Sing You), from Folk Songs of the Americans, 1965, by Albert Lancaster Lloyd. Copyright © Novello & Co., Ltd. International Copyrights Secured. All Rights Reserved. Reprinted by Permission of G. Schirmer, Inc. (ASCAP). English version by Pearson Education, Inc. 60: "John Kanaka" © 2002 Pearson Education, Inc. 64: "The Loco-Motion," Words and Music by Gerry Goffin and Carole King. © 1962 (Renewed 1990) Screen Gems-EMI- Music Inc. This arrangement ©

Index of Songs

and Speech Pieces